TRANSPORTATION RATES AND ECONOMIC DEVELOPMENT IN NORTHERN ONTARIO

N. C. Bonsor

Transportation Rates and Economic Development in Northern Ontario

PUBLISHED FOR THE ONTARIO ECONOMIC COUNCIL BY
UNIVERSITY OF TORONTO PRESS
TORONTO AND BUFFALO

Canadian Cataloguing in Publication Data

Bonsor, N.C., 1944-
Transportation rates and economic development in
northern Ontario
(Ontario Economic Council Research studies ; 7)

ISBN 0-8020-3343-1 pa.

1. Freight and freightage – Ontario, Northern.
2. Transportation – Ontario, Northern – Rates.
3. Ontario, Northern – Economic conditions. I. Title.
II. Series: Ontario Economic Council. Ontario
Economic Council research studies ; 7.
HE199.C2B65   380.5'2   C77-001159-4

This study reflects the views of the author and not necessarily those of the
Ontario Economic Council.

This book has been published during the
Sesquicentennial year of the University of Toronto.

Contents

Acknowledgments

The author wishes to thank Torben Drewes, Robert J. Hanson, and Dan Laprade for the excellent research assistance they provided, and to acknowledge the many helpful suggestions made by Professor John Palmer, University of Western Ontario.

TRANSPORTATION RATES AND ECONOMIC DEVELOPMENT IN NORTHERN ONTARIO

1
Introduction

Economists have long been concerned with determining the underlying causes for the existence of disparities in the level of economic development, as measured by some standard such as the level of employment or income, across the economic regions of a nation.[1] In this context, the role of spatial factors, such as distance and transportation costs, have received some attention. Most of the work relating transportation costs to the level of regional economic growth and development has been highly abstract. Very little attention has been given to the problem of determining the actual level of transportation costs or the effect of such costs on the pattern of regional growth. In the few studies concerned with this, the structural determinants of transportation costs have not been examined in detail.

In Canada, given the extremely large distances between population centres, resources, and production locations, it is not surprising that transportation costs have been an item of major concern. The main purpose of this study is to examine the impact of transportation costs on regional economic development, with special reference to Northern Ontario. There are two important aspects to be considered: first, whether the over-all level of transportation costs exerts a significant influence on regional economic development and, second, whether the existing structure of Canadian freight rates unduly discriminates against specific regions.

1 A good but brief survey of the development of economic thought on regional problems is given by Richardson (1970, 1-14).

Since Confederation freight rates, especially rail rates, have been held by politicians and others to be a prime determinant of the level of economic development of regions not considered economically central. Specifically, where growth has occurred at a slower rate than the national average the transportation costs have been cited as the cause. In an analysis of railroad subsidies in Canada, Darling aptly expressed this view: 'Transportation, having been the decisive factor in creating the Canadian economy, any failure or shortcoming in the functioning of the regional economies has tended to be attributed to transportation, and the remedies for such shortcomings are immediately sought in transportation policy' (1974, 1).

Producers and consumers located a great distance from major markets will have a larger portion of their respective revenues and incomes absorbed by transportation costs than economic agents located adjacent to major markets. Thus most complaints on the level of freight rates have come from producers and consumers located outside the areas of major economic activity.

The development of the attitude that transportation policy is both a cause and a cure for regional ills can be traced to Prairie and Maritime positions on freight rates. Prior to the turn of the century, discontent over freight rates was most evident in Manitoba and was due in large part to the virtual monopoly that the Canadian Pacific Railroad had over for-hire transportation. In 1883, for example, rates charged by the CP for the transport of wheat originating in Manitoba were in some cases double the rate prevailing in Southern Ontario. From Brantford to Montreal, a distance of 403 miles, the rate per 100 lb was 17½ cents, while from Moose Jaw to Winnipeg, a distance of 398 miles, the rate was 34 cents. The differential on long distance rates was also substantial: from Winnipeg to Toronto (1,287 miles) the rate via the CP was 50 cents, while the rate via the Grand Trunk from Ingersoll to Halifax (an almost identical distance) was 31½ cents (Glazebrooke,1938).

The first relief to Western Canada from the high level of freight rates was given by the Crow's Nest Pass Agreement in 1897. In return for a subsidy, the CP agreed to build a line through the Pass and also to reduce rates on some grain shipments and 'settlers' effects.' However, rates on goods other than those covered by the agreement were much in excess of rates in Eastern Canada (Currie, 1967). The differential was reduced in the 1914 *Western Rates* case and gradually eliminated thereafter. Rail rates still evoke considerable criticism from Prairie interests, who maintain that the region is placed at a disadvantage because they are high and discriminatory.[2]

2 See, for example, the comments by Jack Horner on the federal government's proposal to alter parts of the existing transport policy (House of Commons *Debates*, 1975, 119, 154).

In the Maritime region, discontent over the level of freight rates did not become a serious concern until after 1923. Until it was absorbed into the Canadian National system, the Intercolonial Railway, built to give Maritime producers access to central Canadian markets, was operated by the Dominion government as a deficit operation. Beginning in 1912 the rate level, which was significantly below that prevailing in Ontario and Quebec, was increased both absolutely and relatively. Between 1917 and 1920, rates in Eastern Canada increased by over 98 per cent, while in the Maritimes rates increased by about 120 per cent. After full parity in rates between Eastern and Maritime Canada was achieved in 1923, they became an important issue, with the Maritime provinces interpreting the promises made at the time of Confederation as implying rail rates low enough to permit access of regional outputs to central Canadian markets.

In an attempt to offset the competitive disadvantage of a Maritime location, and also the harmful effect on the region of the protectionist tariff policy, the Maritime Freight Rates Act of 1927 was passed. Its main feature was a reduction in rail rates of 20 per cent on local all-rail traffic within the select territory and a similar reduction in the rates for the select territory portion of traffic originating there and destined for other parts of Canada. The Act defined the select territory as the three Maritime provinces plus the portion of Quebec lying east of Lévis and Diamond Junction. The Dominion was responsible for paying the 20 per cent subsidy to the rail carriers.

Although the scope and level of the Prairie and Maritime subsidies have changed since their inception, they still exert an important influence over the structure of Canadian freight rates. In the current interpretation both are intended to reduce the transportation cost disadvantages of groups of producers located in these regions. It can, however, be argued that the Crow's Nest Pass grain rates should be viewed as a loose income maintenance supplement rather than as a measure designed to eradicate the locational disadvantages of Prairie grain growers.

From the perspective of price theory, transportation costs can be treated as arguments in supply or demand functions. Where raw materials, factor inputs, production sites, and consumers are not located at the same point in space, friction arises. This friction can be overcome only by the application of scarce resources to provide transportation services. The effect of transportation costs on consumer demand is shown in Figure 1, on the assumption that the consumer's location in space is given. In the absence of transportation costs, the price line for good X in terms of all other goods M is given by XM, and equilibrium is established at point A. The imposition of a transportation charge on X will lead to a new price line $X'M$ and to a new equilibrium position at point B. If X is not a Giffen good, less of it will be purchased. With the consumer's

Figure 1

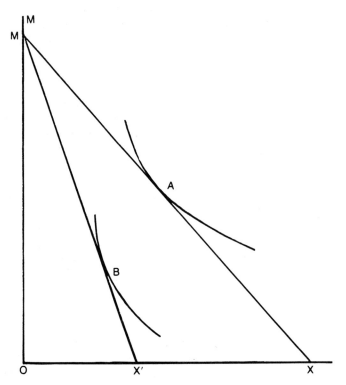

location fixed, an increase in the level of transportation costs will lead to a further downward rotation of the price line and thus to further decreases in the quantity of X purchased. With respect to the demand curve, increases in the level of transportation costs imply a leftward movement along the demand curve for X.

Consider the demand curve for a representative consumer given in Figure 2. We assume that the 'factory-gate' price for the good is set at $0P1$. If the consumer is located adjacent to the production point, and transportation costs in consequence are assumed to be zero, quantity demanded will be $0Q1$. If the consumer is located λ miles from the production point, and if transportation costs are at a rate of t per mile for each unit of output, quantity demanded will fall to $0Q2$, with the producer receiving a price of $0P1$ and the supplier of transportation services an amount equal to $(P1 + \lambda t) - P1$ per unit. (It has of course been assumed that the producer's underlying production function

Figure 2

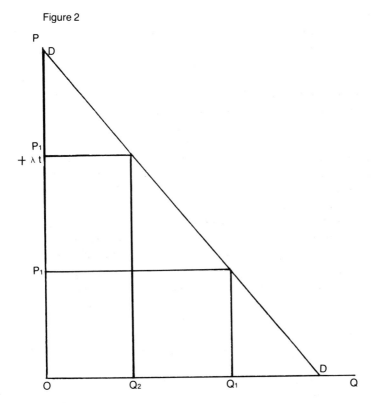

exhibits constant returns to scale. If the production function gives rise to upward sloping marginal and average cost curves, the factory-gate price of $0P1$ will change as quantity demanded changes). Any increase in the level of the transportation rate t or distance λ will lead to a reduction in quantity demanded.

The effect of transportation costs on a producer's ability to compete in markets will depend in part on the underlying shape of the production function, the cost of factor inputs, and the type of market structure. Consider an economy with two centres, A and B, where centre A is large and centre B small. We assume that A and B are separated by a distance of λ miles and that there is an equal availability of all factors required for the production of good X. Factor prices are posited to be the same in both centres, and the production function is characterized by non-increasing returns to scale. If the market for X in centre A is competitive, producers located in centre B will not be able to sell in centre A since, with price set equal to marginal cost (assumed to be the same for both producers), producers located outside of centre A are at a competitive disadvantage because of the presence of transportation costs. If the market in centre B is not competitive, producers located in B can earn a surplus profit equal to the transportation cost between A and B.

When the assumption of equal factor prices in both centres is relaxed, and it is posited that the price of at least one factor is lower in B than in A, the product can be produced in B and sold in A provided the cost differential is equal to or greater than the transportation costs. If producers in centre B are making greater profits than those in A there will be an increase in the level of production in B. In general, the relaxation of the assumptions on the production function and on factor prices can lead to production being increased at A or B.

Transport costs can be thought of as a wedge inhibiting competition between spatially separated economic agents. In a competitive world a producer located in one market area will not be able to sell his output in another market area unless he has some specific cost advantage which can offset the cost of transporting the product. In the context of a typical neoclassical regional model, nodes outside the central region can attract new industry only if payments to factors of production are lower than those prevailing in the central region, unless of course there are specific advantages, such as access to specialized inputs. Since capital is generally assumed to be highly mobile, this implies that payments to factors other than capital must be below the levels prevailing in the centre if the region is to grow.[3]

Even though technology and factor inputs may be equally available across all regions at a given price level, costs may differ across regions because of the presence of agglomeration economies. These economies arise when producers can achieve a reduction in costs by locating adjacent to each other. Agglomeration economies can be divided into three main types: external economies to firms in many industries, economies external to the firm but internal to the industry, and transfer economies.[4] If these economies are important, producers located outside of large nodes will be at a disadvantage compared with producers located in large nodes, unless their payments to factor inputs are lower than those to be obtained in the large nodes. External economies are of course very difficult to measure (see, for example, Isaard, 1956, 182-8). However, if they are present and if transportation costs are in excess of zero, a node of small size will generally be a less attractive locational choice than a larger node unless there are offsetting advantages.

The size of a centre may itself offer considerable advantages in growth opportunities. Thompson (1965) argues that growth creates size, and 'size reacts to restructure the local economy so as to virtually ensure growth at a near

---

3 An excellent treatment of this topic can be found in Anderson (1976a, 1976b).
4 For a detailed discussion of the role of external economies see Guthrie (1955).

average rate.' In brief, it is suggested that growth becomes self-sustaining in large centres. For a centre or region of less than the critical minimum size required for self-sustaining growth, growth can only come about through the attraction of a new export base or the expansion of an existing one. In order to attract a new export base, a region must possess a cost advantage over other regions. Transportation costs will reduce the potential advantage of regions distantly located from major markets.

Where transportation costs are large relative to other factor costs or to market prices, the ability of producers to transport outputs to given markets will be reduced. Transportation costs may thus render some locations uneconomic as production sites. It is not hypothesized that relative rates of economic growth in Canada's regions are the result exclusively of transportation costs, nor that transportation costs are the prime reason for the non-convergence of income levels and employment rates. Factor price differentials, imperfect factor mobility, access to non-ubiquitous raw materials, and agglomeration economies may be of importance.

In many cases, however, transportation costs will be an important determinant of the ability of a region to attract new sources of employment and thus income. In the specific case of Canada, given the large distances between population centres and resource locations, transportation costs can be expected to exert an influence on producer location decisions.

With respect to the Northern Ontario economy, a noticeable feature is the absence of a set of diversified secondary manufacturing industries and a high dependence on two resource-based industries: mining and forestry. In the Northeastern portion, comprised of the districts of Algoma, Cochrane, Manitoulin, Nipissing, Sudbury, and Timiskaming, the most important industry is mining, while in the Northwestern portion, comprised of the districts of Thunder Bay, Kenora, and Rainy River, the forestry and pulp and paper industries predominate. In 1973 the mining industry provided 20,563 jobs in the Northeastern part of the region and 3,667 in the Northwestern portion.[5] It is to be noted that during the period 1966 to 1973, output in the mining industry, measured by tons milled, increased by approximately 25 per cent in the Northeastern region and by 50 per cent in the Northwestern region, while employment in mining decreased by almost 10 per cent in both regions. In Northwestern Ontario the forestry and pulp and paper industries directly employed over 18,000 persons in 1973, with the majority being in the pulp and paper sector.[6]

5 These figures, as well as others pertaining to activity in the region's mineral sector, are obtained from the Ontario Mineral Review (1974).
6 This figure was obtained by using the 1971 Census data and applying the Ontario rate of growth in this industry to the data.

The 1971 Census of Canada reveals that for the major urban areas of Northern Ontario, average family income is above the provincial average and much in excess of that pertaining for major centres in the Maritimes. For Sudbury, Sault Ste Marie, and Thunder Bay, the Census shows average household incomes of $11,990, $10,706, and $10,165 respectively. By comparison, the appropriate figures for Toronto, Hamilton, St John's, Saint John, Fredericton, and Moncton are $11,912, $10,519, $8,488, $9,112, $9,659, and $9,112.[7] In the parts of Northern Ontario outside of the three major centres the level of average income tends to be significantly lower than the provincial average.

Population growth in Northern Ontario has been much slower than the provincial average. Over the period 1966 to 1971, the provincial average increase was 10.7 per cent, but in Northern Ontario only 5 per cent. Population growth in the Northwestern portion of the region during the period was only 0.4 per cent.

From an economic viewpoint, the reliance on a few resource-based industries for a significant portion of total regional employment may lead to an inherent risk of instability. In a report on Northern Ontario development the Ontario Economic Council expresses concern that the reliance of the region on a narrow export base has 'resulted in increased vulnerability to changes in world demand. Cyclical movements in demand and prices ... adversely affect the stability of the many communities heavily dependent on one or, at the most, a handful of economic pursuits' (Ontario Economic Council, 1976, 3).

The regional economy has not managed to diversify greatly from the original narrow expert base. In order for the economy to grow, the region must either increase its share of the existing export-base industries or attract new industries. With respect to the first, it should be noted that the mining, forestry and pulp and paper industries are highly capital-intensive, and in all three productivity has been increasing at a rapid rate. In consequence, while output has been expanding in response to increases in demand, the level of labour input has remained relatively constant in the forestry and pulp and paper industries and has actually fallen in the mining industry. If this high level of productivity gain is assumed present in the future, further increases in demand, or an increase in the region's share of such industries, cannot be expected to lead directly to large increases in the level of regional employment.

It is possible that part of the reason for the region's inability to attract new export activity is to be found in its spatial isolation from major market areas and

7 The data for Moncton and Fredericton are for average family income.

in the structure of Canadian freight rates. Not only are the major centres of Northern Ontario a large distance from the Quebec and Southern Ontario markets (up to 1,000 miles in the case of Thunder Bay), but they are also distant from each other.[8] The region's relatively small population base implies that domestic demand will often not be sufficient to enable producers to take advantage of available economies of scale. Thus in order for a production location in Northern Ontario to be viable for given industries, part of the output will have to be shipped to markets outside of the region. If transportation costs are large in relation to total production costs, and large compared with those in other possible production locations, we would expect them to exert a significant influence on location decisions.

In this study, we concentrate on deriving the absolute and comparative disadvantages due to transportation costs on producer locations in non-central regions. As a first step, the absolute level of transportation costs for the movement of inputs and outputs to and from Northern Ontario will be determined, as will similar information for other regions. It is also necessary to determine whether or not the structure of rates in Canada discriminates against certain regions. For example, a region may enjoy a natural or inherent advantage in the production of a given commodity over all other regions. These natural advantages (and the associated disadvantages of other regions) may have been altered by government- or producer-induced transportation rates.

---

8 The major industries in the regional economy do not appear to display any significant interindustry linkages.

2
Freight rates in Canada:
an overview

For the purpose of this study, three modes of freight transportation are of importance: rail, highway, and lake shipping. Air cargo operations are not included in this study because they account for only a very small proportion of total freight transportation. Transportation by pipeline is excluded because of the specialized nature of this mode; at present the transportation by pipeline of commodities other than oil and gas is negligible.

Before proceeding with the construction and estimation of a model, it is necessary to look briefly at the overall structure of freight rates in Canada.

RAIL RATES

The structure of rail rates in Canada is especially complex. Basically, commodities move under five separable rate categories: open class rates, agreed charge rates, commodity rates, commodity competitive rates, and statutory grain rates. Of the five rate types, agreed charges and commodity competitive rates are designed to meet competition from other transportation modes. Open class rates, commodity rates, and statutory grain rates are not shaped by competition from other modes.

The National Transportation Act of 1967 declares that 'an economic, efficient and adequate transportation system making the best use of all available modes of transportation at the lowest total cost ... [is] most likely to be achieved when all modes of transport are able to compete' (National Transportation Act, 1967, s.3). However, the federal government, through the Canadian Transport Commission (CTC), enjoys a wide degree of control over rail rates. Section 23 of the Act allows the Commission to alter tolls which it finds to be 'prejudicial' to the public interest. The latter being interpreted to be adversely affected if the tolls are discriminatory or at a monopoly level. The Act allows rail carriers a significant degree of flexibility in setting rates and defines 'reasonable' rates as those which range between variable cost and two-and-one-half times this amount. Certain statutory rates, such as those on grain and those authorized by the Maritime Freight Rates Act, are excluded from this rule.

The revision of Section 334 of the Railway Act allows the CTC to require proof that rates are set high enough to cover variable costs. The various costing orders handed down by the CTC, however, indicate that their version of 'variable' cost bears little relationship to the economist's classic definition of 'variable.' The CTC requires that fixed costs, such as some interest expenses, depreciation, and other long-run costs be classified as variable. Agreed charge rates are apparently exempt from the rule that rates are at least to cover 'variable' costs.[1] The Act offers some specific protection to captive shippers: where rates are judged to take undue advantage of a monopoly position, they can be disallowed and new ones prescribed.

OPEN CLASS RATES

Open class rates cover all commodities. The Canadian Freight Classification No. 22 (and supplements) classifies commodities according to a five-digit system. The classification runs to over four hundred pages and groups commodities into nine classes. The rate for each class is expressed as a percentage of the rate applicable to class 100. The second part of the pricing system for class rates is found in the class rate mileage scales, which shows rates for 105 mileage blocks. This means there is a maximum of 105 separate prices based on distance for each class. The blocks are of unequal size, with the smallest being for short-haul journeys.

As an example, the class rates between Thunder Bay and Toronto or Montreal are shown below in cents per 100 lb:

Class	100	85	70	55	45	40	33	30	27
Rate	941	800	659	518	423	376	311	282	254

For a commodity in class 100, such as a typewriter, a computing machine, or parts valued between $1.50 and $5.00 per pound, the cost of transportation will

---

1 Agreed charge rates are authorized by Part IV of the Transport Act of 1938. For a discussion of this point, see Feltham (1974) and Prabhu (1971).

be $9.41 per 100 lb. If the commodity were to fall in class 45, such as oil in barrels or boxed cans, the rate would fall to $4.23 per 100 lb.

The class rates are based on a value-of-service pricing concept and attempt, by discriminating according to what each type of traffic will bear in terms of a rate, to attract the maximum revenue from traffic moving under these rates.[2] Although considerable attention has been focused on the class rates (primarily because they are most visible and easiest to understand), they play only a minor role in the structure of rail rates. In recent years the proportion of total non-grain traffic moving under the class rates has been decreasing. In 1951 the class rates accounted for 12.4 per cent of total non-grain traffic; for 1973 this had fallen to just over 1 per cent.

The reason for the decline in the importance of class rates can be attributed to the growth of competition. With growing competition from highway carriers the ability of rail carriers to discriminate effectively with class rates has been substantially reduced. At the present time, class rates are primarily utilized by shippers with low volumes of freight movements. Essentially, only where alternative rates are unavailable will traffic move under the class rates. The reason for this is clear: class rates in general are more than double those available in other categories. For 1973 the waybill analysis indicates an average revenue per freight ton mile of 4.89¢ for class-rated traffic versus an average of approximately 1.7¢ for all non-grain traffic.[3]

AGREED CHARGES

Agreed charge rates are one of the most important rate categories, accounting for approximately 20 per cent of the total non-statutory grain transportation for the period 1970-3. They were permitted for the first time in 1938. Prior to this, the railways were losing a portion of their volume to highway and steamship carriers. Shippers frequently used cheaper truck or water shipping services during the summer months and in winter sent their freight by rail. Agreed charge rates were introduced in an attempt to make rail rates more flexible in meeting competition. Section 35 of the Transport Act of 1938 defines an agreed charge in the following manner: 'A carrier may make such charge or charges for the transport of the goods of any shipper or for the transport of any part of his goods as may be agreed between the carrier and that shipper: provided that any such agreed charge shall require the approval of the board.'

Although the spread of the agreed charge rates was hampered by the complaints of non-rail carriers and small volume shippers, they are an important

2 A detailed treatment of Canadian railroad rate-making is given in Currie (1967).
3 *Canadian Transport Commission, 1974;* these figures pertain to carload traffic.

part of the structure of freight rates. The rate is negotiated between the carrier and the shipper for a period of one year. They have in common the feature that the shipper must guarantee that a certain percentage of the traffic covered by the agreement (typically 80 per cent) will be shipped under the agreement.[4] If this clause is not adhered to, the shipper is subject to a number of heavy financial penalties. In order to achieve a discount on his shipping costs, the shipper is granting the rail carrier a limited monopoly on his business for a stated time period. A rate agreed between a specific shipper and a carrier is also available to other shippers in substantially the same position.

Under the current legislation, carriers and other persons adversely affected by an agreed charge may lodge a complaint with the minister of transport, who can refer it to the CTC for investigation. Under Section 33 of the Transport Act, the Commission has the following guidelines for deciding on the reasonableness of an agreed charge:

In dealing with a reference under this section the Commission shall have regard to all considerations that appear to it to be relevant, including the effect that the making of the agreed charges has had or is likely to have on the net revenue of the carriers who are parties to it, and in particular shall determine whether the agreed charge is undesirable in the public interest on the ground that it is unjustly discriminatory against any person complaining against it or places his business at an unfair disadvantage or on any other ground, and, if so directed by the Governor in Council in a reference under subsection (2), whether the agreed charge is undesirable in the public interest on the ground that it places any other form of transportation services at an unfair disadvantage.

As an example of an agreed charge, Imperial Oil has a rate agreement for shipping petroleum from points in Ontario and Quebec to points west (this agreement is distinct from a tank car shipping agreement). The rates in force from Montreal to Thunder Bay show a rate of 153¢ per 100 lb for a minimum shipment of 60,000 lbs, decreasing to 147¢ per 100 lb for a minimum shipment of 70,000 lbs. If the same commodity were to be shipped under the appropriate class rate, the rate would be 423¢ per 100 lb.

COMMODITY RATES

Although still important, the percentage of total traffic moving under commodity (non-competitive) rates has been declining. In 1951, for example, 73

4 Some agreed charge rates require a 100 per cent shipment.

per cent of all rail non-grain traffic moved under these rates. For the period 1970-3, the figure was down to between 40 and 44 per cent.[5]

The commodity non-competitive rates are based, as are the class rates, on the principle of charging what the traffic will bear. The rates are intended to provide for the movement of those commodities which, if shipped under the appropriate class rates, could not remain competitive in the market place. In order to attract traffic that could not move under the class rate structure, rail carriers publish a variety of commodity tariffs. The tariffs mainly cover the shipment of low-value bulk commodities, such as minerals and forest and farm products. It will be shown later that with the exception of regions served by water transportation there is little intermodal competition for these products. Economically, the rail carrier enjoys a large cost advantage in moving these products compared with highway carriers. If it is posited that rail carriers have excess capacity, then any rate above 'true' marginal cost which attracts additional volume is economically desirable. If there is excess demand for rail facilities, and if the level of capacity is fixed in the short run, then theory suggests that the levels of rates should be increased. In this circumstance, commodity non-competitive rates would rise above the existing level.

The commodity non-competitive rates either are based on mileage scales (for commodities produced and consumed over a wide geographic area) which apply to a large number of origin-destination pairings or are specific tariffs applying only between a limited number of specified points. The most important feature of the commodity non-competitive rate group is the very low rate per ton mile. In 1973 the average rate for this category was 1.14¢, compared with 4.89¢ for the class rates, 2.26¢ for the agreed charge rates, and 2.14¢ for the commodity competitive rate group. The importance of commodity non-competitive rates varies from region to region, as does the level of these rates. They are most important for intra-western shipments, however, where the average rate in 1973 was 0.97¢.[6]

COMMODITY COMPETITIVE RATES

The 1938 Transport Act, s.23, defines a competitive rate as one applicable when a 'toll or tolls lower than in the standard freight classification be charged between points which the Board may deem or have declared to be competitive points.' The rates were introduced to enable rail carriers to compete with highway and waterway carriers. In contrast to agreed charges, the rates are not

5 Computed from waybill data (Canadian Transport Commission, yearly).
6 Computed from the 1973 waybill data (Canadian Transport Commission, 1974).

named for specific shippers and in consequence do not require the fulfilment of minimum traffic guarantees on the part of the shipper.

The rapid increase in the use of commodity competitive tariffs since 1938 has been surrounded with a great deal of controversy and claims of unjust discrimination, especially from Prairie and Maritime interests. To understand the reason for this, it is necessary to note that one of the features of the Canadian rail rate structure is that a specific commodity, such as steel, may be carried from point A to point B at a total rate per ton cheaper than for an identical shipment from point A to a point intermediate between A and B. In the latter case, the transportation charge is higher in total than for the former even though the distance may be considerably lower. The reason for the differential is that the rate between A and B is a competitive rate which neither applies nor sets maxima for movements intermediate between A and B.

The major complainants have been the provinces of Alberta and Saskatchewan. There are rates between Montreal/Toronto and Vancouver considerably lower than the rates on identical commodities between Montreal/Toronto and Edmonton or Calgary. The reason for this is that competition – in this case ocean shipping between the East and the West coasts – is present or higher on one route than on the other.

Following the 1951 royal commission, the Railway Act was amended to ensure that the rates to intermediate points would not exceed the transcontinental rates by more than 33 per cent. The rail carriers argued that they could not increase the rates on transcontinental routes and remain competitive and if they lowered the tolls to Alberta they would lose revenue. They therefore published agreed charges, which did not come under the 'one and one-third rule,' for transcontinental movements instead of competitive rates. The 1967 Act eliminated this rule, replacing it with the prohibition in s.23 that rates should not bestow 'an unfair disadvantage beyond any disadvantage that may be deemed to be inherent in the location of the traffic.' Such 'disadvantage' can be taken to mean a lack of competition. However, recent examples of through rates being absolutely lower than intermediate rates are still giving rise to charges of unjust discrimination, especially from Prairie interests (see House of Commons *Debates*, 1975, 119, 154).

STATUTORY GRAIN RATES

On an annual basis between 23 and 28 per cent of total rain ton-miles move under rates which are 3¢ per 100 lb below those prevailing in 1889. The Crowsnest Pass agreement of 1897 provided that Canadian Pacific, in return for a subsidy of $3,404,720, would build a rail line between Lethbridge, Alberta, and Nelson, British Columbia, and would reduce the rate on the eastward movement of grain to the Lakehead by 3¢ per 100 lb, effective 1899, as well as reducing rates on the westward movement of 'settlers' effects.' In 1925 the Railway Act extended the coverage of the Crow's Nest Pass rates and elevated them to the status of statutory rates. At present the rates, which are binding on three rail carriers, apply to the following movements: 1/ all shipments of grain and flour moving from the West to the Lakehead, 2/ all shipments of grain and flour moving from Prairie points to Armstrong and West Fort, 3/ shipments of grain and flour for export from Prairie points to the west coast ports and to Churchill.

The rates yield carriers an average ton-mile revenue of 0.48 to 0.5 cents. In consequence, although grain shipments under the rates accounted for 28 per cent of total ton-miles in 1972, they yielded only 9.9 per cent of rail carrier revenues. It should be noted that carriers do not receive any subsidy for losses incurred under the statutory grain rates. Thus if these rates are below the level of marginal cost, the loss must be recouped by cross-subsidization. It will be shown in a later chapter that the grain rates have important direct and indirect effects on railroad pricing.

RAIL RATES: SUMMARY

In Canada it appears that an important ingredient of the structure of rail rates is a value-of-service pricing concept. Thus, rail rates are not strictly determined by the cost of providing any specific service but are largely set by a complex system of discrimination intended to maximize revenue and the contribution to overhead costs.

The importance of each type of rate class and the level of rates in each class show wide variations across regions. On a regional basis, it can be seen from Table 1 that the lowest level of freight rates is for movements emanating from the West. Over 67 per cent of total non-grain traffic originating in the West moves under the commodity non-competitive rates, compared with only 16 per cent in the East and 15 per cent in the Maritimes; 56 per cent of Western traffic, representing the intra-Western movements, is carried at a rate below one cent per ton-mile. It is also interesting to note that when competitive and agreed charge rates are considered, the rates from East to West are 130 per cent and 177 per cent respectively of the West-to-East rate.

HIGHWAY RATES

Intraprovincial highway trucking rates are subject to provincial regulation. The type of regulatory activity varies from province to province, with some provinces

TABLE 1

Non-grain rail freight movements, 1973

| | Rate per ton | | | | | |
| | Maritime | | East | | West | |
	¢	%	¢	%	¢	%
Class rates	4.03	2.2	4.8	2.3	6.2	.22
Commodity rates						
	Mar-Mar		*East-Mar*		*West-Mar*	
Non-comp	2.41	9.12	1.34	5.6	1.07	1.18
Comp	2.88	13.33	1.96	7.98	1.45	1.41
	Mar-East		*East-East*		*West-East*	
Non-comp	1.9	5.3	1.8	8.75	1.28	10.13
Comp	1.48	31.7	2.25	23.28	1.81	11.7
	Mar-West		*East-West*		*West-West*	
Non-comp	1.46	.69	3.05	1.4	0.97	56.01
Comp	1.59	3.28	2.37	20.23	2.38	10.14
Agreed charges						
Mar-Mar	2.48	9.08	2.26	3.67	1.18	0.52
Mar-East	1.37	23.3	2.44	14.79	1.58	3.94
Mar-West	2.88	1.9	2.81	11.93	2.12	4.69

NOTE: Rates are quoted in cents per ton-mile. The percent figure related to the percentage of traffic originating in a region for a given
type of rate.
SOURCE: Based on the 1973 waybill analysis (Canadian Transport
Commission, 1974).

controlling rates directly and some the level of entry into the industry. Using
highly aggregated data, Sloss (1970), McLachlan (1972), and Palmer (1973) have
attempted to measure the effects of regulation on rates. Palmer's estimate,
perhaps the most reliable given the aggregate data, is that de facto regulation
accounts for an upward shift of rates by 2¢ per ton-mile and de jure regulation
by between 0.9 and 1.8¢ a ton-mile.

It will be shown in this study that trucking rates in Ontario and Quebec, two
provinces where the industry is highly regulated with respect to entry, are
significantly higher than in other provinces. Indeed, Ontario rates are the highest
in Canada: a fact not accounted for by cost differentials.

In Ontario, entry into the for-hire trucking industry is controlled by the
Ontario Highway Trucking Board. To acquire a licence for a specific route, the
applicant must either purchase an existing carrier's licence or obtain one from
the Board. The criterion for granting or not granting a licence is that of 'public
necessity and convenience.' From the available evidence, entry into the industry

appears to be very difficult.[7] The Board has no formal power, however, to regulate rates.

With respect to interprovincial trucking, Part 3 of the 1967 National Transport Act (proclaimed 15 May 1970) brings this sector of the industry under the control of the CTC. Previously licences had been granted by the provincial governments. The criterion for the granting of a licence is again that of 'public necessity and convenience.' The Commission has the power to set aside published rates under two general conditions: where existing rates are not compensatory and where rates take undue advantage of a monopoly situation. In addition, the powers under s.23 of the 1967 Act (those relating to rates prejudicial to the public interest) extend to interprovincial highway trucking.

There is a basic distinction to be drawn in regulation between rail and highway carriers. Prior to the 1930s the rail industry controlled a very high proportion of intercity total freight ton-miles. Moreover, it was implicitly assumed by regulators that railroads had many of the features of a decreasing cost industry. Thus as output increased, the average cost of production would decrease. Because of these two factors the rail industry was regulated with respect to both entry and rates. Today, entry into the industry is difficult. Apart from the very heavy capital investment required, the Canadian Parliament directly controls entry for interprovincial routes. In brief, the major aim of regulation has been to protect the 'public' from the assumed monopoly power of rail carriers. As the degree of monopoly power has diminished over time, because of competition from other transport modes, the level of regulation has also diminished.

With regard to the trucking industry, economic theory does not suggest that regulation is required or desirable. From an economic perspective, entry is relatively easy, requiring little capital investment. Since entry is not blockaded, and since there is a high ratio of variable to fixed costs, a rate of return to existing carriers above normal would attract new entrants. In most provinces, however, the for-hire trucking industry is more closely regulated than the rail industry. The consequences of regulation will be discussed in later chapters.

With respect to the classification of highway rates, there is a noticeable similarity to rail rate forms. There is, for example, a class rate structure based on the Canadian freight classification, together with a mileage scale. This, however, tends to be more important in the trucking industry than in the rail industry. In some provinces the regulatory bodies have no power to enforce adherence to any rate scale, while in others a rate scale is fixed by the Board and mandatory for all carriers. In addition, there are rates designed to meet competition from other

7 Information provided by executives of trucking companies.

modes; these take the form of special commodity rates and a loose version of rail agreed charges.

Shippers may be able to lower their highway transportation costs by providing trucking services themselves. In a fully competitive market where price is equal to marginal costs, there will typically by little incentive to do this except in the presence of some specific advantage, such as time savings. The private trucking operation will not be able, legally, to arrange for-hire back-hauls. However, if for-hire trucking rates are in excess of long-run average cost, the incentive to provide own trucking services is increased. In 1972, the federal government estimated that for-hire trucking accounted for 109 million tons of freight, compared with 63 million tons for private trucking.[8]

WATER CARRIER RATES

Given the geographic location of Northern Ontario, it is apparent that water transportation represents a possible alternative to rail and highway transportation for freight movements east of the Lakehead.

Water carrier rates can be classified into two major forms: a class rate structure for package freight based on the rail class rate system and special charter rates. The class rates are priced below rail rates, reflecting the difference between the modes with respect to speed and frequency. The structure, along with various commodity rates, has been designed to assist in the formulation of lake-rail, rail-lake, and rail-lake-rail rates. Shipping companies also enter into long- and short-term contracts for the chartering of whole vessels. The rates charged for such services are not however published. Fortunately, we have been able to obtain some data with respect to cost and rates. These will be presented later.

It can be argued that the importance of water transportation on the Great Lakes and St Lawrence Seaway is restricted to the movement of bulk commodities, such as grain, coal and iron ore. Since the mid-sixties, between 80 and 90 per cent of the Seaway traffic has fallen into the bulk commodity category. In 1971, for example, 34.6 per cent of the total was accounted for by bulk agricultural commodities, and 42.6 per cent by mine products. Package freight was less than 1 per cent of the total. The proportion of mine and grain products for the Upper Great Lakes region is even larger.[9]

8 These figures are contained in Transport Canada (1975). No indication is given of how they were derived.
9 Information on seaway tonnage can be found in the annual report of the Seaway Authority.

For the future, it is hypothesized that the importance of non-bulk shipments will decrease from its present very low levels. With the exception of bulk commodities, containerization of waterborne movements offers considerable cost savings over conventional handling methods. With respect to the Upper Lakes, an investment in container handling facilities could not be economically justified under existing conditions. Compared with conventional port facilities, container facilities are highly capital-intensive. In order to utilize the facilities efficiently, a high rate of throughput is required. No port on the Upper Lakes can generate sufficient volume to warrant container facilities (Schenker, 1969, 1970).

Even if it were possible to show that there was sufficient volume to warrant a container terminal, the physical limitations of the Seaway, coupled with the underlying cost structure of the shipping industry, militate against the use of container vessels. To be able to navigate the Seaway, vessels are restricted to being less than 750 feet long by 25½ feet draught by 75 feet beam. Although lake vessels are typically built to these dimensions, ocean-going vessels are not. The lake fleet cannot of course be operated safely in salt water since they settle too high in the water and their length is out of proportion to their beam. Although ocean-going vessels do traverse the seaway, the present generation of container vessels is excluded from navigating the major portions of it. The reason for this is that almost all container ships built in the last five years have a draught in excess of thirty feet.

The question arises whether or not it would be possible to operate small container vessels on the Great Lakes. A large body of evidence indicates that there are considerable economies of scale with respect to ship size (see, for example, Canadian Transport Commission, 1970; van den Burg, 1969). First, as the size of the ship increases, the capital cost per ton decreases. Second, as ship size increases, the average variable costs also decrease. Thus small vessels exhibit a higher cost per ton carried, both in the short run and in the long run, than do larger vessels. A shipping company official indicated that the resulting increase in cost would not permit waterborne container traffic to be competitive with rail and highway transport, given the present level of rates of the latter modes.

The underlying cost structure of the shipping industry is dominated by the extremely high degree of capital intensity. As an example, the cost of a 30,000-deadweight-ton self-unloading ship in March 1975 was $35 million. We can convert this figure to a daily capital cost by using the following formula for the capital recovery factor:

$$\text{CRF} = r / (1 - e^{-rt}),$$

Where r is the required pre-tax rate of return and t is the assumed life length of the ship. The CRF includes both a rate of return and depreciation.[10] We assume that the life length of the ship is twenty years and that depreciation is straight line. Given the level of corporate profits before tax, a required rate of return of 12.5 per cent can be assumed to be reasonable. This yields a capital recovery factor of 0.136178. Based on a 270-day shipping season, the capital cost per day is $17,652. If the life length is assumed to be twenty-five or thirty years, the daily capital costs are $16,948 and $16,593 respectively. It is difficult to find an accurate figure for variable costs. However, the rule of thumb in the industry is that these are between 25 and 30 per cent of annual capital costs.[11] This figure includes labour costs, fuel costs, and maintenance expenditures. If ports and loading facilities are not suffering from congestion, a round trip between Thunder Bay and Toronto should take approximately 195 hours, including loading, unloading, and refuelling time. Thus, the ship can make 33.7 trips each shipping season. Based on a one-way load with no back-haul (a reasonable assumption in this specific case), the long-run cost per ton is around $6.00. (The figure was achieved by allowing for a scrap value of $4 million at the end of a twenty-year life). Thus the cost per ton mile is approximately 0.63 cents. It should be noted that this is a 'fully allocated' cost, the marginal cost is very much lower than this. In addition, the figure reflects an assumption of zero waiting times for loading and unloading, but on the other hand assumes that costs are based on new construction prices. The actual rates charged will depend on the degree of competition and on the relationship between demand and capacity levels. However, it will be shown that the costs for waterborne transportation of bulk commodities from Thunder Bay are significantly lower — in some cases about half — the prevailing rates by rail.

MARITIME FREIGHT RATES

During the period from 1912 to 1923 the level of freight rates on the Intercolonial Railway had been raised from 80 per cent of the prevailing rate in central Canada to equality. In addition, between 1917 to 1921 the general level of rail rates increased by between 77 and 70 per cent.[12] Thus, during an eleven-year period rates in the Maritimes approximately doubled.

10 This methodology has been used in deriving capital cost factors for aircraft (Keeler, 1972; Bonsor, 1974).
11 Based on confidential information supplied by a company operating lake vessels.
12 For a historical analysis of the maritime freight rate issue see Glazebrook (1938), Currie (1967), and Darling (1974).

The Maritime provinces claimed that the entry of Nova Scotia and New Brunswick into Confederation was made on a promise by the Dominion that the operation of the Intercolonial Railway would ensure access for their commodities to the central Canadian markets. The large rate increases, and the restoration and extension of the Crowsnest Pass rates, led the Maritime provinces to ask, amongst other things, for a permanent rate differential on traffic moving outward from the Maritimes on the Intercolonial portion of the Canadian National system. The Royal Commission on Maritime claims (the Duncan Commission), while noting that freight rates were not the sole cause of depressed conditions in the Maritimes, recommended that the Dominion government roll back Maritime rates to 80 per cent of those prevailing in central Canada.

The Maritimes Freight Rates Act of 1927 provided for a reduction of 20 per cent on all rates on traffic originating and terminating within the select territories and on the select territories portion of outbound traffic originating within the region (except imports). The select territory was defined as comprising the provinces of Nova Scotia, New Brunswick, and Prince Edward Island and the portion of Quebec located east of Diamond Junction and Lévis. The subsidy did not extend to traffic moving from points outside into the select territory, to passenger or express traffic, or to highway carriers. The subsidy was paid directly to the rail carrier by the Dominion government.

The growth of highway and waterway competition led to two problems in the administration of the Act. First, the question arose whether, when railways reduced rates to meet competition, the subsidy should be paid on the normal rate or on the competitive rate. In 1933 the Supreme Court ruled that where, for example, the normal rate was 4¢ per ton mile and the railways had lowered this to 3¢ to meet competition, the 20 per cent subsidy would be paid on the 4¢ rate rather than the competitive rate. Second, in the mid-thirties rail carriers reduced rates on potatoes in the St Lawrence lowlands to meet intermodal competition but did not reduce them in the Maritimes. The Maritime provinces asked the Board of Transport Commissioners to rule that such competitive rates were prejudicial in that they negated the advantages implied by Statute. The Board agreed with the contention that they were required to disallow rates which negated the Statutory advantage, but ruled against the Maritime provinces on the question of fact. The Board stated that whether or not a tariff was prejudicial was a question of fact, a position upheld in 1937 by the Supreme Court. In brief, such questions lay outside the Act and are now a dead issue since they 'present an impossible question of fact' (Darling, 1974).

It is interesting to note that from the late forties highway carriers, who were not eligible for the 20 per cent subsidy, began to have an increasingly large share of intra-Maritime traffic. There is little doubt, however, that the single-mode subsidy inhibited the growth of highway carriers. In 1957, because of rising discontent in the Maritimes, the subsidy was increased on outbound interterritorial shipments to 30 per cent. The MacPherson Commission (1961) recommended that the level of the subsidy should not be increased but that it should be available to other modes, and that the intraterritorial subsidy be eliminated.

In 1969 the Atlantic Regional Freight Assistance Act extended the benefits of the 30 per cent subsidy to truckers on the Maritime portion of outbound traffic. Traffic moving wholly within the select territory by truck was granted an equivalent subsidy to rail traffic in late 1970. The interterritorial subsidy, however, was reduced to 17½ per cent in December 1970, with a further reduction to 15 per cent in 1974, when the subsidy on some selective outbound movements was at the same time increased to 50 per cent.

In 1973, the subsidies paid under the Maritimes Freight Rate Act and the Atlantic Regional Freight Assistance Act came to $14 million and $14.5 million respectively. Since their inception, the summed annual subsidies in current dollars paid under the two Acts up to the end of 1973 totalled $407.6 million. Their effectiveness will be evaluated in a later chapter.

3
The theoretical model

The purpose of this study is to estimate the effect of transportation costs on regional economic development. It is necessary to develop an econometric model to determine empirically the structure of Canadian freight rates. Clearly it is not sufficient merely to estimate the absolute level of transportation costs for the major inputs and outputs of the regional economies. The high level of aggregation implied by this approach will mask many of the important functional relationships in the rate structure. We need to determine how rates vary across different commodities and regions with respect to variables such as distance, weight, value, and degree of intermodal competition. Once the structure of freight rates has been estimated, it can be related to a region's competitive ability to produce and market various commodities. Finally, if the rate structure is found to discriminate unduly against the ability of a region to attract or maintain employment opportunities, policy alternatives can be more meaningfully analysed.

FACTORS INFLUENCING RATE-MAKING

The model to be estimated must have a strong theoretical justification. If the structural relationships are misspecified theoretically, the results of the estimation procedure will have a high probability of being misleading. Thus even statistically significant results will be meaningless if the model is theoretically incorrect. Worse, policy prescriptions made on the basis of 'faulty' empirical results may exacerbate the existing situation rather than alleviate it.

We hypothesize that freight rates, given demand, are determined by three sets of factors: by the cost structures of the carriers, by the degree and type of intramodal competition, and by the degree and type of government regulation of the transport sector. With respect to the structure of cost, it is apparent that there are large differences in the underlying production functions for rail, water, and highway modes. Water transportation is characterized by a high ratio of fixed to variable costs when compared with rail transportation. A similar result obtains when rail costs are compared with highway costs.

In this discussion we are using the terms 'fixed' and 'variable' costs in their traditional economic meanings: costs related to inputs whose levels cannot be changed in the short run and costs related to inputs whose usage can be altered in the short run. This division into fixed and variable costs bears little relationship to the 'variable' costing technique imposed on rail carriers by the CTC in order R6313. This order requires that some costs which are really long-run rather than variable, such as some interest expenses and depreciation, be treated as variable. It is perhaps not generally recognized that the rule contained in the 1967 National Transportation Act that all rates must cover variable cost implies a minimum rate of marginal cost *plus* a portion of fixed costs.

It is also important to note that divisibility in terms of owner-supplied additions to capacity varies widely across modes. For example, to add units of capacity to the lake shipping fleet requires an addition of 30,000 tons.[1] In the rail mode, boxcars can be added with an increase in capacity of forty tons per car, while for highway carriers the minimum capacity addition is approximately twenty-five tons.

The difference in the structure of economic costs between modes has significant implications for rate making. Figure 3 shows relative total cost functions for the three modes on the restrictive assumption that variable costs are a function of distance only and are linear. For the distance between zero and $D1$, highway carriers have a built-in advantage over other modes because of the lower level of fixed costs per trip. Between $D1$ to $D2$, rail carriers have an advantage over highway and water transportation. For distances greater than $D2$, water transportation has lower costs than the other modes.

Clearly the actual positions in the real world will not be as clear-cut as this. Costs depend on the volume, weight, and type of commodity as well as on distance. We would expect to find areas of overlapping and thus a range in which modes are competitive. Figure 3, however, does indicate that the initial disadvantage of high fixed costs per trip is offset by lower marginal costs as distance increases, and vice versa.

In the short run, rail and water carriers have a greater latitude in which to set prices than do highway carriers. In Figures 4A and 4B, cost curves have been

1 Based on minimum costs for alternate sizes of ships.

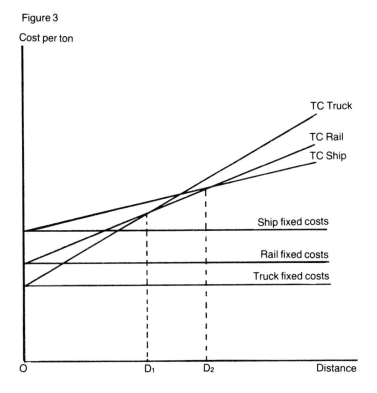

Figure 3

Cost per ton

TC Truck

TC Rail

TC Ship

Ship fixed costs

Rail fixed costs

Truck fixed costs

O   D₁   D₂   Distance

drawn on the assumption that we are not dealing with the case of decreasing cost industries. Figure 4A presents a stylized set of cost curves for rail and water carriers, where q refers to the level of output measured in tons, with distance held constant at some level. (Though it may be inappropriate to treat both modes in the same diagram since cost structures are dissimilar, it is done for simplicity). In the short run, rail and water carriers can set a price as low as $P1$. For highway carriers (Figure 4B), the minimum short-run rate is much higher, at $P2$. If there is excess capacity present, rail and water carriers can feasibly add to their total profits (or decrease their total losses) by offering any rate in excess of $P1$. As can be seen from Figure 4B, highway carriers cannot offer a rate below $P2$. It can also be seen that rail and water carriers have a greater ability than highway carriers to differentiate across consumers and commodities below the long-run price.

The second set of factors which help determine the structure of freight rates is the degree and type of intermodal competition. Consider three routes, A, B, and C. On route A there are rail, water, and highway modes; on route B rail and

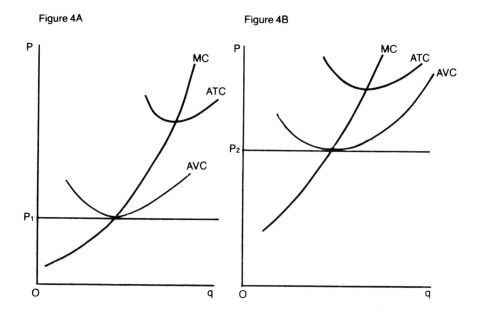

Figure 4A   Figure 4B

highway; and on route C rail only. In the absence of all regulation except anti-trust policies to prohibit collusion, rates on route A will tend to be lower than on routes B and C. For commodites moving a long distance we would expect competition between rail and water modes to lead to rates which approach a competitive level, especially if there are no barriers to entry into the water transportation sector. Competition between trucking firms and the rail mode will similarly operate on less than long-distance movements.

On route B, the rail carrier has an effective cost advantage over highway transportation for all except short-haul movements. If the rail carrier has some measure of excess capacity he can attract traffic from highway carriers by cutting rates. On commodities and distances for which the fully allocated cost of rail transport is higher than for highway transportation, the marginal cost of rail transportation may be lower. Thus, in the short run the rail carrier can capture a portion of traffic which would have moved by highway if fully allocated cost pricing had been in effect. Predatory pricing — setting rates below marginal cost to drive a competitor out of the market — will not generally be successful. In the long run, entry into the trucking industry is relatively easy from an economic viewpoint. Thus, if highway carriers are driven from the market and the rail carrier raises his rates and earns monopoly rents, new entrants will be attracted into the trucking industry.

On route C, where the rail carrier has a monopoly, price will typically be higher than on routes A and B. Since there is no competition, the rail carrier can

Figure 5

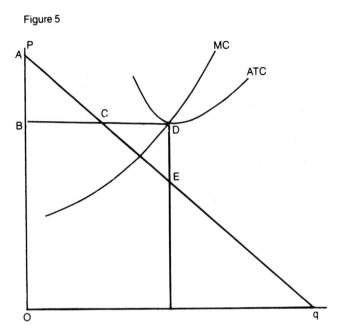

effectively practise value-for-service pricing, that is, differentiate between consumers and commodities based on demand rather than on cost.

The ability to discriminate between consumers, locations, and commodities is a function of the level of competition. Economic theory suggests that the more competitive the markets, the lower will be the level of price discrimination. Discrimination, where it is not based on cost differentials, is an outgrowth of some degree of monopoly power. But it is not correct to assume that discrimination is necessarily without benefits.[2] In some instances, discrimination is necessary before the output of a non-subsidized private producer will be greater than zero. Consider the case presented in Figure 5, where the average total cost curve is above the demand curve. In the long run there is no single price at which output will be forthcoming. If the producer is able to discriminate, output will be set at $\bar{q}$ if the area *abc* is greater than the area *cde*. In brief, price discrimination leads to a transfer of consumer surplus to the producer.[3]

2 Perfect price discrimination (first degree in Pigou's terminology) may be required for optimal allocation; see Anderson and Bonsor (1974).
3 Pure discrimination arising from the exercise of monopoly power cannot be judged as necessarily suboptimal even if it is not required for positive output. In the case of a captive shipper who is a monopoly producer, the outcome may lead to a transfer of producer surplus from the shipper to the carrier.

In Canada, the major criticisms of price discrimination in the transport sector have come from the Prairie Provinces and have concerned railroad pricing.[4] One of the methods suggested to eliminate price discrimination is to have all rates set at the level of fully allocated cost (see Wilson, 1962; Roberts, 1965). Ignoring the very real problem of determining an adequate method for assigning the joint and common costs to specific types of traffic, it is doubtful whether the measure would greatly help those it is intended to benefit. The problem with suggestions of this nature is that the role and influence of competition is completely ignored. Consider a carrier providing rail services on two routes, one with a high degree of effective competition from other modes and the other with no competition. In the latter case we assume that rates on a given haul are higher than for an identical haul on the competitive route. We assume that the introduction of fully allocated cost pricing will initially equalize the two rates by increasing the price on the competitive route and lowering it on the other. However, the carrier may be unable to compete on the competitive route. If the maximum rate that the carrier could charge on the competitive route was in excess of short-run marginal cost but below the level of long-run average total cost, any increase in the rate would be economically unjustified and would lead to a loss of traffic. If some of the carrier's costs for the two routes fall into the joint or common category, the portion previously covered from revenues on the competitive route would have to be met out of revenues from the non-competitive route. Thus, the level of rates would increase on the latter route.

Where there are no regulations limiting competition, we would expect to find rates, and the degree of price discrimination, lowest where there is effective competition. The presence of alternative modes does not by itself lead to competitive rates: if there is a substantial difference in costs between a high-cost and a low-cost mode, the latter may earn more than normal profits. Entry of new carriers in response to the high level of profits depends on whether or not there are barriers to entry. If entry is blockaded, as it is for example in the rail industry and to a lesser extent in some provincial highway sectors, high long-run profits may not be eliminated.

The third set of factors influencing rates is the type and magnitude of regulation of the transport sector. In theory, regulation is required where a monopolist or a cartel is capable of using its power to earn large economic rents. Typically, most objectives of regulating industry can be accomplished by anti-trust policy. In some cases, however, regulation of entry into an industry and price and output levels is required, The classic case is that of a decreasing-cost industry, where the presence of more than a single producer will

---

4 The debate on the proposed revision of federal transport policy is a good example of this (House of Commons *Debates*, 1975, 119, 154).

lead to higher than optimal prices. If entry is restricted, the power of the monopoly producer to set prices must also be restricted.

Philosophically, regulation can be viewed as an attempt either to simulate or to stimulate a competitive outcome with respect to price and quantity. In the context of the transportation sector of the Canadian economy it is very difficult to make a strong case for the need for a high level of regulation. Many parts of the industry which are now highly regulated do not possess the characteristics of decreasing cost, nor are there natural barriers to entry. Air and highway transport are cases in point: the cost function in both modes is relatively flat with respect to output (measured by the number of trips), and the underlying production function has coefficients indicating approximate constant returns to scale (Straszheim, 1969; Meyer et al., 1959). Even in the rail sector, where it has typically been assumed that regulation is required because of increasing returns, studies of the US rail system indicate few economies of scale (Borts, 1954, 1960; Griliches, 1972).

In recent years the role and effectiveness of regulation in the transportation sector has come under increasing scrutiny from economists. The general consensus has been that deregulation would lead to a decrease in the over-all level of transportation costs and rates and result in an improvement in welfare.[5] Moore (1975) aptly expresses this by stating: 'it is widely recognized that regulatory commissions usually develop tendencies to protect the industries they regulate from competition.' This can be most clearly seen in Canada in federal regulation of air carriers and the operation of some provincial highway boards. In brief, regulation may well lead to higher rates than would have prevailed if competition had been permitted.

THE RATE FUNCTION

If sufficient data were available for all transport modes, it might be feasible to generate statistically meaningful cost functions. Rates could then be compared with cost and an index of cross-subsidization by route and commodity type could be constructed. Only in the case of air transportation is the disaggregation of costs fine enough to permit this approach. This study concentrates on determining the structural relations in the rate function. In general, we expect all transport rates to be composed of two components: the fixed costs of each journey and the variable cost of the journey. In its simplest form this can be expressed as follows:

$$R_i = a_i + b_i d \quad (i = 1, 2, ..., N), \tag{1}$$

5 A large bibliography can be found in Phillips (1975).

where R_i is the rate for transporting commodity i measured in tons, a_i is a constant, and b_i the slope of the rate line with respect to distance d. The fixed costs in equation (1) can be thought of as the station costs, mainly the costs associated with loading the commodity, and will vary across modes and commodities. For example, it is probably less costly to load an open car with 60,000 lb of crude material; such as coal, than to load a boxcar with 60,000 lb of manufactured commodities. Clearly, the level of a will be independent of distance.

The variable cost with respect to distance is measured by b_i, which is thus the marginal cost of transporting a given commodity expressed as a function of the length of haul. The rate structure will be dependent on the relationship between a and the shape of the marginal rate function for each mode. If the marginal cost of transporting a commodity were constant with respect to distance, the total trip cost would increase by a constant amount as d increases. If, however, there are 'economies' associated with distance, the marginal cost curve would slope downward and the total trip cost would increase at a decreasing rate.

One of the most frequently mentioned characteristics of freight rates is that the average cost per mile to the shipper decreases as length of haul increases. The term 'tapering' has been applied to this. It should be noted that a declining average rate curve can arise for two reasons. First, if the marginal cost per mile is a constant, the average rate curve would be hyperbolic in shape: the 'effective' rate per mile would decrease since the fixed costs are being 'spread' over a larger distance. Thus as distance increases, the average cost per mile will asymptotically approach b_i. It is important to note that any rate structure with a constant marginal rate and a vertical axis intercept in excess of zero will lead to a decreasing average total rate per mile. Second, if the marginal rate is a decreasing function of distance, both the average and marginal rate curves will fall, with the latter lying below the average.

The shape of the rate curve with respect to distance is important for the purposes of this study. If $\partial^2 R/\partial d^2$ is negative (implying a decreasing marginal cost function), the impact of distance on transportation costs is lessened. Consider two manufacturers shipping identical products to market and located 100 miles and 200 miles from that market. The relative disadvantage of the product locations depends on the shape of the marginal rate curve. If it is decreasing at an increasing rate, the total transportation costs for both producers could be identical, or even lower for the most distant producer. In brief, if the marginal rate does decrease, the locational disadvantages associated with distant points will be reduced compared with the situation involving a constant marginal rate function.

In the literature it has normally been assumed that highway transportation is characterized by a marginal cost curve which is constant with respect to distance

(Palmer, 1973; Fair and Williams, 1975). This, combined with the constant cost component, leads to a hyperbolic average cost curve (Palmer, 1973). There has been little empirical validation of this. The rates actually charged cannot be taken as either supporting or undermining this hypothesis since other variables, such as the level of competition and regulation, have an important impact on rate levels. If highway rates are not set competitively, short-haul rates – where there is little competition from other modes – will be higher than optimal. The average rate in this case will decrease as distance increases, in part because of intermodal competition. However, there does not appear to be any convincing reason for assuming that marginal cost per mile falls as distance increases. We thus assume a constant marginal cost function with respect to distance.

For rail and water transportation the data indicate that as distance increases the average rate per ton-mile decreases. For rail, the decrease is such that average rates drop sharply over the distance from zero to four hundred miles. In order for marginal cost to fall with distance there must of course be economies with respect to distance. This could come about because of a decrease in fuel consumption, less wear and tear on equipment, or increased efficiency in using labour. Discussions with railroad engineers and technical personnel have suggested that such economies are not present. For rail, the assumption of a constant marginal cost curve with respect to distance will therefore be made. For lake shipping, the available evidence does not allow us to indicate whether the marginal cost curve is constant or falling.

Besides distance, we would expect shipment weight to exert a significant influence on the structure of freight rates. In many instances the total cost of moving a full truck, rail car, or ship, as against a half-full one, will be roughly the same for any given distance. Carriers can thus offer lower rates per ton-mile as weight increases up to the maximum capacity weight of the transport unit. In Figure 6 the marginal transport cost per car mile is shown as a constant with respect to Q. Dividing this by Q yields the curve MC/Q, which declines until the carrying capacity of the transport unit (car, truck, or vessel) is reached. In a non-competitive situation not all the advantages of increasing weight will be passed on to the shipper.

It is necessary to distinguish carefully between weight and volume. As the frequency of shipments of any given size increases, it is probable that the cost per unit (per ton-mile or car-mile) will decrease. The reason for this is that carriers are better able to utilize equipment, meaning less 'downtime,' increased productivity, and lower 'gearing-up' costs. This can be seen in its most sophisticated form in the unit-train concept. It is generally agreed that the cost savings which flow from unit-train usage are large: a CP rail study (1975) on grain transportation indicates that costs would decrease from $254 million to

Figure 6
Rate

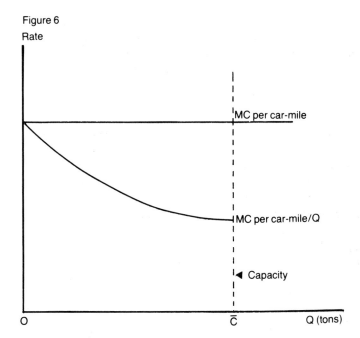

$159 million by switching to unit trains. Such savings are only available to shippers or groups of shippers with very high volumes and/or to those located on high-volume routes.

The effect of weight and volume on the rate structure should be measured separately. The first, weight, can be determined directly from the data. For rail, highway, and water transportation the data indicate that the rate per 100 lb decreases as weight increases. In some cases an increase in weight of 40 per cent leads to a rate reduction as large as 20 per cent. Shippers able to take advantage of this by consolidating shipments into large blocks (or able to use the services of freight forwarders) can enjoy significantly lower freight costs than shippers who are unable to consolidate.

The volume factor is more difficult to measure. We were not able to obtain returns for a sufficiently large number of individual shippers to make direct measurement possible. However, the use of agreed charge rates are generally only available to high-volume shippers. By the use of a dummy variable for agreed charges, some of the effects of volume on rates can be estimated.

Across commodities, the weight/density ratio may be an important explanatory variable of differences in rates. For example, a rail car or highway truck capable of carrying a 40,000 lb load may, with some commodities, be fully loaded at only 20,000 lb. If the marginal cost of carrying an extra 20,000 lb is very small, the rate per ton-mile will be lower on goods with a high weight per cubic foot than on goods with a low weight per cubic foot. Thus the rate per 100 lb for commodities such as cotton wool will be higher than for commodities such as iron ore. Unfortunately, an adequate measuring rod for this variable could not be determined.

Thus far we have assumed that the rate structure is determined by cost. But the transport sector is not perfectly competitive, so that rates will depart from marginal cost. In many instances regulation has actually inhibited the feasibility or effectiveness of modal and intermodal competition. Regulation thus allows the existence, or amplifies the presence, of imperfections which can lead carriers to increase rates above marginal cost by taking advantage of the ability to discriminate across commodities, shippers, and origin-destination pairs. One area where there may be measurable systematic discrimination is in the value of the goods being shipped. We have already shown that revenue will be greater if carriers are able to discriminate by pricing according to value-of-service. If rate-makers do not have detailed knowledge of the demand elasticities of commodities they are carrying, they are likely to approximate this by assuming that demand elasticities are roughly inverse to the value of the products (Meyer and Wohl, 1970). Thus, in the absence of effective competition, carriers may be in a position to extract a greater revenue per ton-mile from the shipper if the value of the commodity is high than if it is low. We are assuming that the demand for transport services with respect to rates is related to the market value of the commodity and to the share of total costs attributable to transportation expenses. The lower transport costs are as a percentage of total costs, the more inelastic will be the demand for transportation services. A doubling of transport rates on a million-dollar computer is not likely to bring about a change in demand for transport services, since transport costs are a very small portion of total costs. But a doubling of rates on commodities such as iron ore, where transportation costs are a relatively large portion of total costs, would probably lead to a large decrease in the demand for transportation.

Olson (1972) has recently tested the hypothesis that US highway trucking rates discriminate between commodities by basing rates on the values of the commodities being shipped. Using 1966 data for Middle Atlantic conference class rates, she concludes that such rates 'do seem to be explained by price discrimination. It appears that motor common carriers not only still practice value-of-service pricing but do so in a surprisingly systematic manner. Cost of hauling and commodity price explain the class rate structure much better than either variable alone can' (Olson, 1972, 2). Value of the commodity will therefore be included as an argument in the rate equation.

The rate equation for transporting the ith commodity by any given mode can be written as

$$\frac{R_i}{D_i} = a_i + b1 \, \frac{1}{D_i} + b2 \, \frac{1}{W_i} + b3 V_i + b4 \, \text{AC}, \tag{2}$$

where R_i is the rate for the ith commodity, D_i the distance transported, W_i the weight of the ith commodity, V_i the value of the ith commodity, and AC a dummy variable for agreed charge rates. The dummy variable is used in an attempt to capture some of the effects of volume on rates.

It should be noted that the form of equation (2) does not allow for the effect of differences in costs across regions on the level of rates. For example, one of the reasons for rate differences across regions for any given mode may be due to differences in the cost of factor inputs, an influence that may be especially important in the case of highway transportation. A carrier located in one region may face higher costs for fuel, labour, and capital equipment than a similar carrier located in a different region. Specifically, a carrier located in Northern Ontario can be expected to face higher prices for trucks than a carrier located in Southern Ontario; fuel prices may also be higher. Any differential in labour costs can of course either reduce or increase the differentials caused by vehicle and fuel costs. In relation to total shipping costs, we hypothesize that such cost differentials across regions are relatively small for highway carriers. First, the vehicle price differential will be small in relation to total truck cost but will increase as distance from Southern Ontario increases.[6] Prices of gasoline and diesel fuel in the Prairie provinces are lower than in other provinces, with the lowest prices being in Alberta and Saskatchewan.[7] Most of the price differentials in this connection are due to differences in the levels of provincial taxes on motive fuels. The available statistics on payments to labour in the highway trucking industry indicate that wages are considerably lower in the Maritime and Prairie provinces than in Ontario and Quebec.[8] To a large extent the differences across regions in the major components of highway trucking costs can be assumed to be of an offsetting nature.

6 Partial evidence of this can be found in Wilson and Darby (1968, 9-12) for the case of passenger automobiles. It is normal in the motor manufacturing industry to quote prices FOB the plant.

7 The level of provincial prices for gasoline and diesel fuel can be found from the Statistics Canada publications on prices and price indexes (Statistics Canada, 62-002). The tax per gallon on motive fuel is given in a Statistics Canada publication on Canadian tax rates (Statistics Canada, 68-201).

8 Labour cost data are contained in Statistics Canada (72-611).

There is insufficient statistical information on railways to permit an analysis of regional cost differentials. However, it would seem likely that such differentials would be small, especially as labour unions in this industry bargain for wages on a national basis.

An important variable so far ignored is the effect of back-hauls on rates. In a competitive situation the levels of rates on a specific route would be lower if volume was the same in both directions than if the traffic was predominantly one-way. Consider a rail line running only from A to B. The movement of a train from A to B will result in a return journey from B to A. Assume that the cost equation can be written as $C = a + bd$, where a is $100 per train, b is $1, and d is 100 miles. In the absence of a back-haul, the cost of transportation from A to B is equal to $100 plus $200 ($b$ times 200). If there is a back-haul, the total cost for the two way movement is $400 – an addition of only $100 over the one-way movement. Since the trip from A to B inevitably results in the marginal cost of the return trip, joint costs arise. Such costs are not traceable to the production of a specific trip. If the carrier is a profit-maximizer and able to charge $300 from A to B, he will accept traffic for the back-haul at any rate in excess of the loading charges a. Typically, the joint costs will be assigned to different hauls on the basis of demand elasticity. If the shipper of goods from B to A is charged a rate equal to $200, and if there is competition, the rate from A to B will tend to be lower than in the absence of a back-haul.

In Canada, especially with rail transport, there is an identifiable imbalance in traffic flows, which takes two forms: the major flow is East to West, and superimposed on this is a major flow to large centres from small centres. As an example of this, the Commodity Flow Analysis for 1973 (Canadian Transport Commission, 1974) reveals that, on the basis of the sample, 14.7 million tons of freight originated in the Maritime region. Of this, 2.3 million tons were forwarded West. However, 4.7 million tons were received from the West. Data were derived on a province-to-province basis for the ratio of originating to terminating traffic. In the process several modifications to the data were made, the most significant of which concerned grain traffic. In 1973 Ontario received 13.16 million tons of grain from the West, most of it originating in Saskatchewan. If the data were computed with grain included, this would mean that 9984 carloads of traffic originating in Saskatchewan terminated in Ontario, while only 299 carloads originating in Ontario terminated in Saskatchewan, indicating a high probability of cars originating in Ontario obtaining a revenue-producing back-haul from Saskatchewan. This must be modified since the grain trains are operating in a manner similar to a unit train and car sets are not broken up. With respect to non-grain traffic, only 550 carloads originated in Saskatchewan and terminated in Ontario.[9]

In theory, it is probable that carriers will be motivated to secure revenue traffic for the minor flow direction by offering rates lower than those prevailing on similar movements in the major flow direction. If rail cars are returning empty, any rate which can attract back-haul traffic will be profitable as long as it is in excess of the station costs and the additional marginal costs of hauling full rather than empty cars. In some situations, however, it may be more profitable to have cars returning empty than cutting rates to fill them. If a high percentage, say 70 per cent, of returning cars are loaded, the rate reductions required to fill the remaining cars may be so large that over-all revenue will drop. If the price reductions can be restricted to the marginal units, rate reductions designed to increase flows in the minor direction may be profitable. If the rate reductions must apply to all traffic, inframarginal as well as marginal, and if the demand curve is relatively inelastic, rate reductions may lead to a drop in revenue.

To allow for the effect of back-hauls on rail rates, the variable for distance can be restated as $1/D - (1 - B) D$, were D is distance and B is the probability of a back-haul. Values for B were derived using data for interprovincial carload flows. In a fully competitive situation it can be hypothesized that as B approaches 1, the rates for similar hauls (with respect to volume, weight, distance, and type of commodity), would converge. Several alternative expressions for incorporating the effect of unequal traffic flows on rates will also be derived and tested.

9 These data were compiled from the Commodity Flow Analysis (Canadian Transport Commission, 1974).

4
An analysis of
transportation freight rates

In this chapter we seek to determine the relative impact of transportation costs on the inputs and outputs of the regional economy and whether such costs are higher or lower than those obtaining for other regions.

Given the limited time and budget involved, it was not possible to include all rail, highway, and water rates in the data base. The Canadian Freight Association Tariff 500, which shows commodity rates for All Rail, Rail and Lake, Rail, Lake and Rail, and Water and Rail in force from stations in Eastern Canada to Western Canada is, for example, over five hundred pages in length. This tariff by itself would yield over two thousand rates. In addition, there are numerous other commodity tariffs and agreed charge rates in force as well as highway and water rates. Even if it were possible to include all rates, the results would be misleading because there is no detailed information available on traffic actually moving under each rate.

The Canadian Transport Commission publishes aggregate statistics for carload rail traffic broken down by province.[1] For the purpose of this study, the level of disaggregation permitted by this data is not sufficient. Data allowing disaggregation below the provincial level is not available in a usable format.[2] Rate data for this study was obtained by surveying rates actually in force during the summer of 1975. For rail, rates were obtained from the Canadian Freight Association

---

1 These data are only available for a limited number of centres (Canadian Transport Commission, 1973).
2 Some data are available from Statistics Canada for major-centre highway flows, though the number of centres covered is very limited (Statistics Canada, 53-006).

and the two major Canadian rail carriers. In the case of highway transport, rates were obtained from the provincial highway traffic associations and from individual carriers. A detailed description of the data and sources is given in appendix A.

Approximately 2,450 separate cases are included in the rate sample. Inclusion of a case was determined by the need to be able to measure rate differentials meaningfully across commodities and regions. As nearly as possible, cases were chosen to be representative of regional commodity flows by for-hire transportation. For movements originating in Northern Ontario, a high proportion of the traffic can be classified as either raw materials or intermediate goods. In contrast, a high proportion of in-bound shipments can be classified as for final consumption purposes. Also, a large proportion of out-bound traffic by rail is moving under agreed charge rates, because of competition from other transport modes, and because volume is comparatively high.

Statutory grain rates, rail, and package freight class rates have been excluded from the main data base. Statutory grain rates are based on neither cost nor the degree of competition prevailing in the transport sector but are set at a predetermined level by forces outside of the transport sector. Because of the very low level of such rates (an average of 0.48 cents a ton mile), they would, if included in the data base, produce a significant downward movement in the over-all level of rail rates for movements originating in the western provinces. We do, however, hypothesize that they influence the over-all level of rates for rail movements of a non-grain nature, an effect analysed in appendix B. Rail and package freight class rates have been excluded from the data base because only an extremely small percentage of total traffic moves under these rates.

In recent years several studies have been directed at determining the effect of transportation costs on a region's well-being. All of them have been hampered by a lack of appropriate data. In a study prepared for the government of Saskatchewan, Wilson and Darby (1968) attempted to assess the importance of transportation charges on products shipped to and within the Prairie Provinces and on the shipment of agricultural products out of the region. Using the 1965 waybill analysis they computed ratios to show the relative cost of transportation to the delivered wholesale price of inbound commodities. Noting that 'in spite of considerable arbitrariness in their derivation, we believe the ratios to be relatively reliable indicators' (12), they found that the ratio varied dramatically across commodities, with the highest value being for coal − between 40 and 60 per cent − and the lowest for manufactured commodities − typically below 10 per cent. They concluded that 'in spite of the relatively high rates on goods coming into the Prairies from Central Canada the total contribution of freight costs to delivered prices is surprisingly low.'

In a study comparing manufacturing industries in Nova Scotia with those of Quebec and Ontario, George (1970) considered the effect of freight rates on the cost of production in Nova Scotia. Using data collected by survey, George found that the median figure for product transportation costs as a percentage of total production costs was 3 per cent. If all of the output of the surveyed plants were to be shipped to Central Canada, the figure would rise to 5.3 per cent. Using highly aggregated data, George concluded that these costs were 150 per cent of the corresponding costs for an Ontario/Quebec location. Thus the cost disadvantage due to a location in Nova Scotia of a manufacturing plant shipping to Ontario-Quebec is 2.6 per cent of total production costs. George noted that his figures in this part of the analysis were based on assumptions which 'put the Nova Scotian situation in the worst possible light' (92). The Economist Intelligence Unit's (1967) study of transportation in the Atlantic provinces found that transportation costs (the cost of bringing materials in and shipping the final product) varied between 2 per cent and 15 per cent of total cost. For many secondary manufacturing plants, transportation costs were believed to be approximately 5 per cent of total costs.

In Northern Ontario a very high proportion of regional output, excluding that which is purely of a service nature and consumed locally, is in the form of raw and semi-finished commodities. In addition, the major market areas for such commodities are located a considerable distance from the site of production. Given the low value per ton for such commodities, we should not be surprised to find that the ratio of transportation costs to wholesale prices is relatively high.

In Tables 2 and 3, product transportation costs are shown for a sample of outbound commodity movements by rail and highway modes for shipments originating in Northern Ontario. Column 2 refers to the Standard Industrial Classification (SIC) code for the commodity being shipped, column 3 to the distance the commodity is being transported, column 4 to the average rate per ton mile in cents, and column 5 to the ratio of transportation costs to the wholesale value of the commodity. Tables 4 and 5 present similar information for in-bound shipments. The rate shown for each case is the actual average rate per-ton-mile available for the specific movement. Rate data were obtained for individual agreed charge and commodity rates, and as such the rates are not 'average' rates in the sense of being taken from the waybill analysis. (The problem which arises when the waybill data is used in this connection is that rates for any commodity group are the average rates for all movements in the group. Thus, where commodities are moving under various rate forms – class, agreed charge, and commodity rates – the average rate per ton-mile is the average for all rate forms and similarly for distance. The use of such data masks the actual level of rates.) In each instance the average rate per ton-mile has been

TABLE 2

Sample cases for rail traffic originating in Northern Ontario

Case	Commodity	Distance	Rate	Rate/Value
1	236	95	2.84	5.50
2	238	311	2.25	17.59
3	231	85	4.23	8.43
4	337	479	2.96	4.09
5	444	658	2.37	6.75
6	336	190	5.47	4.44
7	336	618	2.29	6.30
8	336	486	2.51	5.21
9	336	634	2.23	6.07
10	446	548	2.55	6.02
11	336	20	47.00	4.01
12	336	820	1.82	6.42
13	338	1619	2.08	18.45
14	338	1753	2.09	20.09
15	338	1339	1.91	8.28
16	445	505	3.08	6.98
17	341	270	5.18	6.36
18	339	1509	2.21	11.48
19	339	266	2.78	2.54
20	338	776	2.68	6.72
21	338	1189	2.10	8.08
22	255	150	4.29	0.18
23	351	455	3.56	6.61
24	341	1080	1.66	8.62
25	442	1971	2.57	46.26
26	236	170	4.23	10.50
27	444	731	3.17	3.95
28	337	1758	4.72	25.79
29	337	675	5.65	11.40
30	446	2615	1.74	18.53

taken for the lowest weight classification for which the rate applies. In most cases lower rates were available for increased shipment weights, implying that the ratios in column 5 could be lowered by a small amount in instances where shippers are able to take advantage of this cost saving.

The rates available to producers in any given area are in part a function of the degree of intermodal competition. Agreed charge rates, for example, are only available to high-volume shippers on routes where there is competition for the products being shipped. Similarly, commodity competitive rates are available only where inter-modal competition is present. Thus the rate data in Tables 2 to

TABLE 3

Sample cases for highway traffic originating in Northern
Ontario

Case	Commodity	Distance	Rate	Rate/Value
1	331	380	2.77	5.48
2	331	495	2.66	6.86
3	331	410	2.57	5.48
4	331	640	2.43	8.10
5	331	695	2.64	9.56
6	339	597	3.24	7.76
7	448	405	5.92	10.81
8	452	375	3.89	0.95
9	338	445	5.92	5.17
10	339	650	3.78	14.27
11	339	647	3.43	12.88
12	339	619	3.39	12.18
13	351	1415	2.37	12.87
14	351	1255	2.42	11.64
15	351	1195	2.05	10.04
16	351	900	2.28	8.41
17	351	1255	1.88	12.13
18	337	435	4.32	5.41
19	339	585	2.90	6.80
20	337	375	5.01	5.41
21	339	545	4.29	9.37
22	339	743	3.44	14.86
23	338	440	2.86	4.07
24	452	300	4.80	0.94
25	339	558	3.47	7.76
26	331	600	2.20	6.85
27	331	970	1.75	8.83
28	351	1415	2.51	13.63
29	351	1348	2.64	13.63
30	331	970	2.16	14.95

5 will reflect this. For comparative purposes, the type of information contained in Tables 2 to 5 has also been obtained for traffic originating in other regions. These data are shown in Appendix A, Tables A1 to A6.

For rail shipments originating in Northern Ontario, the rate/value ratios appear to be relatively moderate, with the majority falling into the 4 to 7 per cent range. Although the results are not directly comparable with those obtained in other studies, there is a large degree of conformity. Although the ratios for any given commodity increase with distance, the rate of increase in many cases is

TABLE 4

Sample cases for rail traffic terminating in Northern Ontario

Case	Commodity	Distance	Rate	Rate/Value
1	354	690	2.81	8.27
2	354	815	3.41	11.85
3	964	1740	3.22	12.80
4	333	1429	2.47	27.65
5	333	1713	2.06	27.65
6	341	850	2.11	8.62
7	338	844	3.81	17.58
8	442	731	2.65	17.86
9	444	846	4.51	5.79
10	444	994	4.16	6.20
11	354	1087	4.58	6.32
12	351	1500	4.61	28.26
13	337	731	4.95	10.80
14	336	1024	5.25	22.70
15	446	846	4.51	15.52
16	446	811	3.27	10.80
17	353	1014	7.10	16.40
18	353	900	7.64	15.67
19	338	1091	7.02	37.06
20	338	286	12.07	16.35
21	338	65	7.38	2.32
22	338	170	4.23	3.42
23	341	1188	4.64	27.72
24	341	1095	3.85	20.20
25	351	1064	6.50	28.26
26	351	1119	3.75	17.15
27	446	994	4.16	16.82
28	338	319	4.20	27.65
29	342	130	3.38	1.32
30	333	1656	2.13	27.65

small. In the case of woodwork and building components (Table 6) it can be seen that as distance shipped increases from 190 to 486 miles, rate/value increases from 4.44 per cent to only 5.21 per cent, and similarly as distance increases from 486 to 820 miles the ratio of rate/value increases from 5.21 to 6.42 per cent. This tendency was most apparent for commodities produced in more than a few locations, suggesting that railroads were constrained in their pricing policy by the need for commodities to remain competitive in selling markets.

TABLE 5

Sample cases for highway traffic terminating in Northern
Ontario

Case	Commodity	Distance	Rate	Rate/Value
1	331	225	3.71	4.33
2	331	196	5.09	5.03
3	331	385	3.11	6.23
4	252	215	10.88	1.12
5	252	435	10.98	6.44
6	252	250	10.64	3.54
7	945	445	4.40	1.81
8	945	665	3.96	2.45
9	945	525	4.00	1.95
10	945	245	8.00	1.81
11	945	465	5.67	2.45
12	945	325	6.46	1.95
13	945	212	9.24	1.82
14	433	365	5.53	4.53
15	433	580	5.13	6.68
16	494	215	4.37	9.78
17	494	435	3.86	17.50
18	494	250	4.32	11.24
19	441	496	3.70	4.56
20	354	1215	3.65	19.68
21	354	1035	3.86	17.73
22	337	180	7.44	3.85
23	337	265	5.73	4.38
24	428	435	11.17	3.56
25	339	450	4.35	7.84
26	339	370	4.05	6.00
27	339	545	4.29	9.37
28	469	1140	4.00	6.08
29	464	345	8.00	1.18
30	464	942	7.19	2.91

The average rate per ton-mile is typically higher for rail movements
terminating in Northern Ontario than for movements originating there. It will be
shown later in this chapter that this result stands when the full data set for
Northern Ontario rail rates is examined. A high proportion of traffic from
Northern Ontario moves under agreed charge rates, whereas a much lower
proportion of in-bound traffic moves under such rates. In consequence, the
rate/value ratios for terminating traffic tend to be higher than for out-bound
traffic.

TABLE 6

Rail rate/value ratios for woodwork
and building components

Distance	Rate/Value
20	4.01
190	4.44
486	5.21
618	6.30
634	6.07
820	6.42

With respect to highway rates, the rate/value ratio for in-bound shipments was, for a majority of cases, between 1 and 5 per cent. For a wide range of manufactured commodities the ratio was around 1.5 to 3 per cent. These ratios do not appear significantly different from those applying to other non-central regions. For highway traffic originating in Northern Ontario, the rate/value ratios were significantly higher than the ratios on in-bound shipments, in part because of the relatively lower value of out-bound shipments.

Product transportation charges on the present range of regional outputs do not appear higher than those in most other regions. However, most regional output is directly related to the region's natural resource base. For a producer of secondary manufactured goods shipping his output to Southern Ontario, his total transportation costs will in many cases be much higher than for a similar producer located in Southern Ontario. Not only does the finished product have to be shipped to market but also many of the needed inputs will have to be shipped into the region because of the region's narrow manufacturing base. Thus total transportation costs will be higher for the Northern Ontario location than for the Southern Ontario one.

The question arises as to the actual level of transportation costs and the structure of such costs across transport modes and regions. For the econometric portion of this study a large number of equations are estimated. These can be divided into two main groups: those concerned with the structure of inter and intraregional freight rates and those concerned with the structure of rates across commodity categories.

DISAGGREGATION BY COMMODITY GROUP

The rate function was estimated for a number of distinct commodity groups for both rail and highway modes. The data set contained sufficient observations to allow estimation across nine commodity groups, most of which pertain to crude or fabricated materials.

For each mode and commodity group, the following equations were estimated:

$$R/D = a + b1\left(\frac{1}{D}\right) + b2\left(\frac{1}{W}\right), \tag{3}$$

$$R/D = a + b1\,(D) + b2\,(W), \tag{4}$$

where R/D refers to the average rate per ton-mile, D is the distance shipped in miles, and W is the shipment weight for which the rate applies, measured in pounds. The variable for value of the shipment has been eliminated because value will be approximately constant per unit of weight within any commodity group.

Although it has been hypothesized that the appropriate specification with respect to distance and weight is an inverse one, equation (4) was also estimated, primarily so that the results of the two specifications could be compared. For rail and highway modes, the residuals obtained from equations (3) and (4) were examined. Palmer (1973) has shown that forcing data for average rate per ton-mile and distance into a linear framework for the highway mode can lead to the existence of a hyperbolic bag beneath the regression line[3] (Figure 7). For the highway mode a plot of the residuals against distance for the linear specification revealed the presence of such a bag. Indeed, for almost all equations, the residuals formed a very tight compact bag. With respect to weight, the residuals were also plotted; although the pattern was not as striking as that obtained for distance, the residual plot did show the existence of a loose bag beneath the regression line.

For the rail mode the plot of residuals against distance showed a fairly tight but small bag for the linear specification. In the case of weight the residuals did not reveal any very striking pattern.

The results for rail and highway modes are shown in Tables A7 and A8. One of the most noticeable features of the rate structure is that in most cases the average rate per ton-mile is lower for rail movements than for highway movements. The results indicate that weight and distance travelled are both lower for highway than for rail movements. As distance increases past some point, rail transportation rates become lower than truck rates for given

---

3 Figure 7 has been taken from Palmer (1973). For a discussion of residual examination, see Draper and Smith (1966).

Figure 7

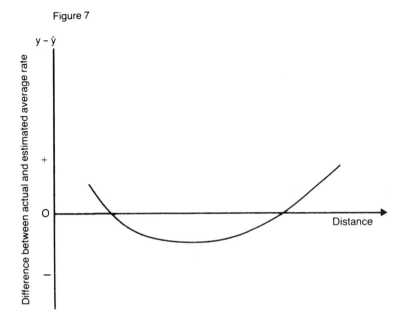

commodities. The advantage of rail transportation stems from the lower line haul costs compared with truck transportation; the disadvantage stems from the higher level of fixed costs per trip. Thus as distance and weight increase, the rail carrier rates decrease faster than truck carrier rates.

The results for the highway mode (Table A7) are relatively good. The postulated inverse relationship yielded far better results than did the linear relationship. In all but one case the coefficient for distance was statistically significant and of the expected sign. The coefficient for weight, however, was statistically significant in fewer cases than the coefficient for distance. Within any commodity group the variation in shipment weight revealed by the raw data is relatively small. This probably accounts for the poorer results. On an aggregate and regional basis, where the weight variable shows greater fluctuation, the coefficient for weight is statistically highly significant. As was expected, the results for the commodity breakdown show that the relative size of the distance coefficient, compared with that for weight, is greater for highways than for rail.

The disaggregation by commodity group for the rail mode yielded fairly predictable results. The lowest rates per ton-mile across commodities were found to be for those in crude form (crude wood and ores). As the stage of production increases, the rate also increases because of several factors. First, the fixed costs associated with loading and unloading are less per ton for crude materials than for finished or semi-finished commodities. Second, both weight and volume of crude commodity movements are higher per separate trip than for manufactured goods. This implies that, because of economies associated with weight and volume, the rate per ton-mile is lower than for other commodity groups. Third, the market value per ton of crude commodities is generally lower than for finished or semi-finished goods. This means that the rail carrier has a reduced ability to extract revenue from the shipper of crude commodities compared with shippers of manufactured goods. In addition, insurance costs will of course be higher for manufactured goods than for crude commodities. The data in the 1973 Waybill Analysis support the above observations; grain, mine, and forest products accounted for 61 per cent of total rail ton-miles and manufactured goods for only 29.1 per cent. Yet in terms of revenue generated, manufactured goods accounted for 51 per cent of total revenue.

DISAGGREGATION BY REGION

In order to determine whether or not there are significant differences in the level and structure of freight rates across regions, the data were disaggregated to permit equations to be estimated on a regional basis. For the rail mode, equations were estimated for fourteen separate origin-destination pairs. For highway traffic, twelve separate origin-destination pairs were examined.

For the rail mode, the following basic equation was estimated:

$$R/D = a + b1 \left(\frac{1}{D}\right) + b2 \left(\frac{1}{W}\right) + b3 \left(\frac{1}{V}\right) + b4. \text{AC}, \tag{5}$$

where R/D is the average rate per ton-mile in cents, D stands for the trip length in miles, W for shipment weight in pounds, and AC is a dummy variable for agreed charge rates. We expect the coefficients for distance and weight to be positive and for value to be negative, implying that the average rate per ton-mile decreases as distance and weight increases. The agreed charge dummy variable should have a negative sign. The results obtained for equation (5) are shown in Table A9.

The coefficient for distance was of positive sign and statistically significant in all but two cases. The distance coefficient for movements originating in the select territory region destined to the East and West regions was not significant. This result is probably due to the influence exerted by the subsidy payments made under the Maritime Freight Rates Act. As was shown in chapter 2, rail carriers receive a subsidy of 30 per cent of the 'normal' rate on the select territory portion of traffic destined for other parts of Canada. Thus as soon as traffic moves out of the select region, the rate per ton-mile would show a sudden increase. The manner in which the subsidy is calculated makes it extremely difficult to construct a dummy variable to take account of this.

With respect to the weight variable, equation (5) was estimated with weight specified in both linear and inverse form.[4] The coefficient for weight was significant in more cases with the inverse than with the linear specification. As can be seen from Table A9, the coefficient was of the postulated sign and statistically significant in all cases. Thus, as both shipment weight and distance increase, the average rate per ton-mile decreases.

In half the cases, the coefficient for $1/V$ was statistically significant and of the postulated negative sign. This of course indicates that as the value of the shipment increases, the average rate per ton-mile also increases. In the case of shipments originating in the West destined for the East, the coefficient was statistically significant but of the wrong sign. In other cases, the coefficient was negative, but not statistically different from zero.

The dummy variable for agreed charge rates showed the postulated negative sign and was statistically significant in half the cases. We should not expect to find the agreed charge dummy variable significant for all regions. Table 1 showed that these rates are most important for shipments originating in the Eastern region and least important for shipments in the Western region when measured as a percentage of total traffic. The results from the regression analysis tend to reflect this situation. The coefficient for this variable was significant for movements originating in the Eastern region. In particular, the coefficient was very large for traffic originating in Northern Ontario. To see whether or not this result would hold for a disaggregation of Northern Ontario into Northeastern and Northwestern subregions, separate equations were estimated. In both cases the coefficient was negative and statistically significant.

In an attempt to obtain an improvement in the over-all results, several alternative formulations were constructed and estimated. First, a dummy variable for manufactured versus non-manufactured shipments was added to equation (5). It was hypothesized that carrier costs would be higher for shipping a manufactured commodity a given distance than a non-manufactured commodity of equal value. The dummy variable was statistically significant and of the expected sign in half the cases. However, the improvement in goodness-of-fit was negligible in most instances.

The probability of obtaining back hauls was included in the regression model. However, this tended to lead to poorer over-all results than those obtained with

---

4 An examination of the residuals revealed that a better fit was obtained with the weight variable specified in inverse rather than linear form. Similarly, a better fit was obtained for the value variable in inverse as opposed to linear form.

equation (5). This may suggest that carriers are not motivated to lower rates on traffic in the minor-flow direction, perhaps because demand is not elastic.

It is apparent that rail rates are not equal across all regions. At an aggregate level, rates on shipments originating in the Western region are significantly lower than rates on commodities originating in the Eastern region. The average rates per ton-mile obtained from the 1973 Waybill Analysis (Table 1) show this clearly, as do the results from the regression analysis. However, some of the difference in rate levels can be ascribed to the nature of the traffic since a high proportion of total bulk movements originate in the West. A detailed examination of the raw data revealed some instances where the rate for East-to-West movements was very different from the rate from West-to-East. For example, the East-to-West rate for a commodity in the edible category was 1.1062 times the rate for the West-to-East movement, with weight the same but the East-to-West distance being 323 miles greater. In other cases, where the East-to-West distance and weight were both greater, the rate per ton-mile was 1.124 times the West-to-East rate.

For highway transportation, the following equation was estimated:

$$R/D = a + b1\left(\frac{1}{D}\right) + b2\left(\frac{1}{W}\right) + b3\left(\frac{1}{V}\right), \qquad (6)$$

where R/D is the average rate per ton-mile, D the distance transported in miles, W the shipment weight in pounds, and V the shipment value. The results are shown in Table A10.

The coefficient for distance was statistically significant and of the expected sign in half the cases, indicating that average rate per ton-mile decreases as distance increases. The coefficient for value was of the expected sign and statistically significant in only five equations; in only three equations was the variable for weight significant.

For shipments originating in Ontario and Quebec, the results were much better than for shipments originating in the West and the select territory. The data set was examined in detail to see if a reason could be found for this. The observations for shipments originating in Ontario and Quebec display a much greater variability with respect to distance than do the observations for the other regions. In the case of Ontario and Quebec, the sample is divided fairly evenly between short, medium, and long trips. The trip length for movements originating within other regions tends to be bunched together and thus does not permit sufficient variability for the meaningful measurement of the regression equations.

In general, there is less uniformity in highway rates than in rail rates. One of the reasons for this is that in many provinces the regulation of carriers does not require that all licensed firms offer identical rates. The operation of rate bureaus does, however, tend to limit the diversity of intercompany rates in many provinces. As an example of wide rate diversity, the rate on steel pipe and tube from Sault Ste Marie to London, Ontario, was 5.92 cents a ton-mile for shipments moving in 40,000 lb loads. In comparison, the rate per ton-mile for plywood moving in 40,000 lb loads from New Liskeard to Georgetown was 2.9 cents a ton-mile. On shipments originating in Calgary destined for points in Ontario and Quebec, the rate per ton-mile for similar commodities moving in 40,000 lb loads was between 2.058 cents and 2.12 cents a ton-mile.

The results of the analysis in this chapter will be discussed in chapter 6 in the context of regional economic development in Northern Ontario.

5
Subsidies and regulation

This chapter assesses the potential impact of granting transportation cost subsidies to producers located outside major market areas. It will be shown that the effect of such subsidies is in part determined by the nature and extent of modal and intramodal competition in the transport sector. Thus, the effect of regulation on competition among carriers will be examined.

Canada, along with most other western nations, has attempted to stimulate the rate of economic development and growth in regions where the level of income or of employment has been significantly below the national average. All such attempts can be viewed as aimed at altering the rate of growth that the market mechanism would have yielded. Five basic methods are employed: subsidies to output, subsidies to capital, subsidies to labour, transportation subsidies, and direct government investment.

The programmes administered by the Department of Regional Economic Expansion (DREE) typically attempt to stimulate regional economic activity by means of capital subsidies. If the prime objective is to raise the level of employment, capital subsidies are generally considered less efficient per dollar of government expenditure than a subsidy which is either neutral in its impact on relative factor proportions or biased towards labour inputs. This has been shown by Borts and Stein (1964) and Archibald (1972). The analysis by Woodward (1974A, 1974B) suggests that DREE programmes are inconsistent with the primary objective of increasing employment.

Woodward suggests that a viable alternative may be found in transportation subsidies.[1] In the Canadian economy, given the large spatial distances involved

---

1 A formal analysis of transportation subsidies is given in Woodward (1973).

between the major market areas of southern Ontario and Quebec and the 'problem' regions, a transportation subsidy may be effective in eliminating the disadvantageous position implied by distance. Theoretically, a subsidy to transport costs has no bias with respect to the optimal level of factor proportions. It can be thought of as a special case of an output subsidy. Thus, given the typical assumption on the shape of the underlying production function of the representative firm, it will have less effect on the employment level than would an equal subsidy on labour inputs. A transportation subsidy taking the form of a fixed percentage of transportation costs will not be neutral across all producers since the subsidy will have an unequal impact on producers of different products at a given location and also on producers of a given product at different locations.

A flat rate percentage subsidy of 10 per cent will tend to have a greater impact on the output of industries for which transportation costs are a significant portion of total costs than where they are only a small part. In general, a transportation subsidy of this type will yield a greater benefit to industries which are heavily resource-oriented (where transport costs are a relatively large proportion of total costs) than for secondary manufacturing industries (where transport costs are much smaller). Similarly, producers located the greatest distance from the market will derive more benefit than those nearby.

A universal transportation subsidy available to all producers in a given region possesses certain disadvantages. Assuming that it is not absorbed by the producer of transportation services through higher freight rates, a large part of the subsidy may be used to increase the level of producer surplus. This could arise if the producer has some degree of monopoly power or faces an inelastic supply curve for factor inputs. Where the transportation sector has non-competitively determined prices, it can be shown that at least part of the subsidy will be used to increase the level of transportation rates.

THE EFFECTIVENESS OF TRANSPORTATION SUBSIDIES

In Canada the transportation sector of the economy is heavily subsidized. Subsidies take two general forms: direct subsidies based on a measure of output, such as ton-miles, and indirect subsidies, such as the provision of overhead infrastructure (highways, airports) with user charges being less than costs. The present level of direct subsidies can be relatively easily determined. However, it is more difficult to measure the level of indirect subsidies. Darling (1974) has estimated that in 1973 direct subsidies amounted to $345 million (excluding a $21.6 million subsidy on feed grain). Haritos (1975) argues that total subsidies to the transport sector are considerably in excess of this figure.

This part of the analysis is concerned with determining the effectiveness of direct transportation subsidies in relation to regional economic development. At present, the subsidies granted under the Maritime Freight Rates Act and the Atlantic Region Freight Assistance Act can be construed as having the primary aim of reducing the locational disadvantages of producers located in the Maritime region. As was stated in chapter 2, the combined cost of subsidies paid under these Acts in 1973 was in excess of $28 million.

In theory, rail rates on commodities moving from the Maritimes westward should be lower than the rates on similar commodities moving in-bound to the Maritimes, and this for two reasons. First, the subsidy is available only with respect to intraterritory shipments and for the Maritime portion of out-bound movements; it is not available on in-bound movements. Second, the data on rail commodity flows (Canadian Transport Commission, 1974) indicate that the ratio of in-bound to out-bound carload traffic is 1.454. This implies that railroads have an incentive, if they are competitive, to lower rates on out-bound movements in order to achieve revenue on what would otherwise be a sizable non-revenue-producing back-haul.

In recent studies, George (1970) and Mohring (1974) have argued that the subsidies paid on applicable Maritime rail traffic have not generally resulted in lower rates to shippers. George, using waybill data for selected years between 1949 and 1962, argues that rates on intra-Maritime traffic were higher than rates on intra-Eastern traffic; thus rail carriers were receiving substantially higher revenues per ton-mile on the former than on the latter. It should be noted, however, that George does not take into account the average weight of shipments in each region.

Mohring advances the proposition that, despite subsidies, rates on traffic in-bound to the Maritimes are 'definately substantially greater than those which would arise under competition' (Mohring, 1974, 290) and that much of the subsidies are not passed on to the shipper. It should be noted that Mohring's data are highly aggregated, so that this may mask some of the effects of the subsidy on the rate level.

In order to assess the probable impact of the Maritime subsidies it is necessary to disaggregate the available data. Table 7 shows the level of rates in 1973 for inter and intra-regional shipments moving under agreed charge rates; Table 8 provides similar data for commodity competitive rates. In both cases, the data were derived from the 1973 waybill analysis. It is necessary to recall that we have shown that rates per ton-mile for given commodities decrease as both distance and weight increases.

With respect to agreed charge rates, analysis of the data in Table 8 reveals a considerable difference in rates between shipments moving from the Maritimes

TABLE 7

Agreed charges

		Miles	Tons	Rate ($ per ton-mile)
Maritimes to	Maritimes	178	51.4	2.48
	East	797	42.7	1.37
	West	2617	19.2	2.88
East to	Maritimes	1019	33.7	2.26
	East	241	52.9	2.44
	West	1938	25.6	2.81
West to	Maritimes	3184	41.9	1.18
	East	2345	36.1	1.58
	West	345	51	2.12

TABLE 8

Commodity competitive

		Miles	Tons	Rate ($ per ton-mile)
Maritimes to	Maritimes	105	50	2.88
	East	806	24.1	1.48
	West	2741	31.7	1.59
East to	Maritimes	809	31.0	1.96
	East	324	45.6	2.25
	West	1961	26.0	2.37
West to	Maritimes	3057	33.9	1.45
	East	2071	28.6	1.81
	West	345	47.9	2.38

to the East (1.37¢ a ton-mile) and shipments moving from the East to the Maritimes (2.26¢ a ton-mile). The East-to-Maritimes average rate is 64 per cent higher than the average rate for movements in the reverse direction. This differential cannot reasonably be accounted for by differences in weight and distance. It is of course difficult to ascertain how much of the differential is due to traffic flow imbalance and how much to the subsidy. From the data available, it is very difficult to determine the amount of subsidy paid on any specific shipment since the subsidy is computed on the basis of 30 per cent of the normal rate, not the agreed charge rate. Thus, if the 'normal' rate for the Maritime portion of the trip was 3¢ per ton mile and the agreed charge rate was 2¢, the subsidy would be 30 per cent of 3 cents. The rail carrier would therefore receive 2¢ + 0.3 (3)¢ a ton-mile.

The Maritime-to-Maritime rate for agreed charge traffic is not appreciably different from the rate for East-to-East movements. When weight and distance differences are taken into account, the rates appear to be almost identical.

With respect to commodity competitive rates, the rate on Maritime-to-East traffic is approximately 45 per cent lower, after adjustments have been made for the difference in shipment weight, than the rate for East-to-Maritime traffic. The rate on West-to-Maritime movements is not greatly different from the rate of movements in the reverse direction. In the case of non-competitive commodity rates, the rate level on East-to-Maritime movements is lower than the level for the reverse movement.

The analysis of the aggregate data for agreed charge and commodity competitive rates, which account for over 82 per cent of rail traffic originating in the Maritime region, leads to two general conclusions. First, there is little evidence that rates on intra-Maritime traffic are significantly lower than rates on intra-East shipments. Thus rail carriers are receiving a much higher revenue per ton-mile on intra-Maritime traffic, because of the subsidy, than on intra-East traffic. Second, rates on out-bound traffic to the Eastern region are lower than on traffic in-bound from the Eastern region. It is not possible to determine how much of the rate differential is due to the imbalance in traffic flows and how much to the subsidy.

The major problem with subsidies of the type granted to the Maritime region is that the incidence is difficult to determine or control. The existing subsidy on Maritime freight can be thought of as an open-ended negative *ad valorem* tax on the output of the transportation carrier. The degree to which the subsidy is passed to the shipper in the form of lower rates will be determined by the degree of competition in the transport industry, the elasticity of demand for transport services, and the shape of the cost curve facing the provider of transport services. The effect of the subsidy on a monopoly supplier is shown in Figure 8.[2] Technically, the Maritime freight subsidy is paid as an addition to the carrier's total revenue. Prior to the subsidy, the average and marginal revenue curves facing the supplier are *DC* and *DB*. As Mohring shows, an *ad valorem* subsidy will result in a shift in the average and marginal revenue curves to *AC* and *AB* respectively. (In Figure 8 *AC* is constructed on the assumption of a 30 per cent subsidy, thus *AC* is 1.3 times *DC*.) If we assume that the industry displays decreasing marginal costs, the marginal cost curve in Figure 1 is appropriate. In

2 For the formal derivation of this see Mohring (1974).

Figure 8

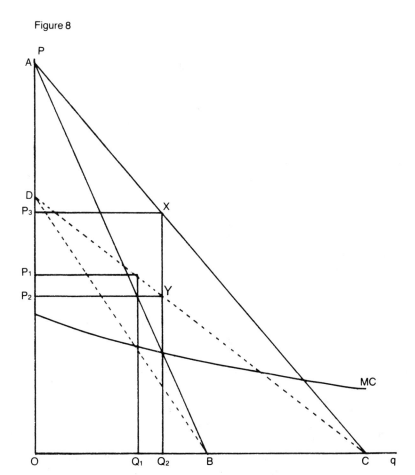

the absence of a subsidy, a profit-maximizing producer would set quantity equal to $0Q1$ and charge a per unit price of $0P1$. (If the carrier is a discriminating monopolist, the analysis will hold across all separate markets). With the subsidy, the profit-maximizing level of output is equal to $0Q2$ at a price to the shipper of $0P2$. The supplier receives a subsidy equal to 1.3 times $0P2$ – equal to the distance XY – for a total price of $0P3$. Under these circumstances the full amount of the subsidy is not passed on to the shipper. If the marginal cost curve is horizontal within the range of outputs being considered, price to the shipper would not drop even to the level shown by $P2$. Mohring also argues, correctly,

Figure 9

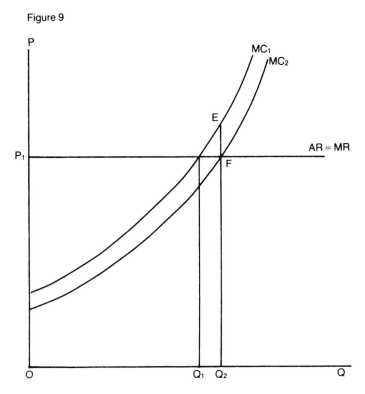

that if the subsidy were directly paid to the shipper rather than to the supplier, the result would be the same with total price set at $P3$.

Consider the case of a competitive producer located in centre A selling his output in a competitive market located at B. If transportation costs are zero, his profit-maximizing level of output, shown in Figure 9, is $OQ2$ at a price of $OP1$. We now introduce a transportation cost per unit of EF, which causes the marginal cost curve to shift upward from $MC2$ to $MC1$. This leads the profit-maximizing level of output to fall to $OQ1$. A subsidy equal to EF per unit will, in the long run, lead to an increase in output to $OQ2$, providing that the transportation sector has competitively determined prices. The cost of the subsidy is equal to EF times $OQ2$. If the transportation industry has some monopoly power in price determination, output will not increase by as much as $Q1$-$Q2$, since part of the subsidy will end up as an addition to profits earned by the transport sector.

Consider the case of a monopolist producer who receives a flat rate unit transportation subsidy. Prior to the subsidy (Figure 10) output is at $OQ1$ with

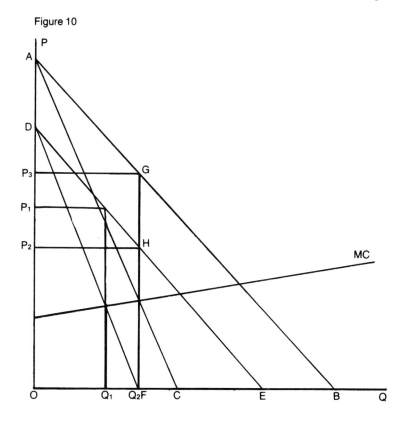

Figure 10

price set at $P1$. A unit transportation subsidy – assuming a competitive transportation system – would shift the demand and marginal revenue curves upward from DE and DF to AB and AC. The result of the subsidy is that output is increased to $0Q2$, with the subsidy worth GH per unit to the producer; the market price falls to $OP2$.

The effect of transportation subsidies on output and prices will be determined by the elasticity of supply and demand curves facing shippers, the degree of competition in the transport sector, and the shape of the carriers' cost curves. In general, the greater the degree of monopoly in the transport sector, the less effective will subsidies be in increasing the level of output. In the case of a monopolist producer facing a monopolist supplier of transport services, the effect of a transportation subsidy aimed at increasing output will probably be small.

A subsidy on transportation costs designed to decrease the disadvantages of producers locating outside major market areas will not necessarily be passed on to the intended recipients. Thus a subsidy paid to the producer of transportation services will not necessarily lead to benefits to shippers commensurate with the size of the subsidy. A similar situation prevails even if the subsidy is paid directly to the shipper. As with taxation, the actual incidence of the subsidy will typically not be the same as the intended incidence.

REGULATION AND RATES

The question arises whether the deregulation of surface for-hire transportation would lead to lower transportation costs and thus reduce the competitive disadvantages of producers located in non-central economic regions.

From an economic viewpoint, the prime aim of governmental regulation of business activity can be thought of as an attempt to simulate or stimulate a competitive set of prices and quantities in those markets where competition is not sufficiently vigorous to ensure an optimal allocation. The classic view of regulation is as a mechanism designed to afford the public at large protection from the possible abuses of market power. In a recent article on the economic theory of regulation, Stigler argues that 'regulation is acquired by the industry and is designed and operated primarily for its benefit' (1971, 3).

A growing body of empirical evidence indicates that regulation not only fails in its function of protecting the 'public at large' but also directly leads to a serious loss in economic welfare by promoting higher than optimal prices.[3] With respect to for-hire surface transportation, Moore (1975) estimates that the economic loss from regulation of US surface transportation in the 1960s was between \$3.7 and \$8.89 billion. Although estimates of this nature are crude, they show that between 15 and 30 per cent of revenue generated in surface transportation could be 'pure waste.'[4] However, a convincing case has been made that regulation of for-hire transportation generates a large number of costly inefficiencies.

The level of regulation of the for-hire surface transportation sector is lower in Canada than in the United States. The National Transportation Act of 1967 effectively removed a large portion of rail traffic from restrictive rate regulation. In practice, the legislation allows rail carriers to set rates on traffic (other than on statutory grain traffic) anywhere between the variable cost of the movement and two-and-one-half times this amount. Rail carriers therefore have a wide range of discretion in setting rates over about 70 per cent of their revenue traffic.

3 For the specific case of surface freight transportation, an excellent survey is given in Moore (1975).
4 For a discussion of such estimates see Moore (1975).

To cast some light on the question of railroad deregulation, it is useful to classify rates in two types: those set to meet competition from other transport modes (agreed charges and commodity competitive rates) and those set in the absence of competition from other transport modes (class rates and commodity non-competitive rates). In the absence of strict regulation we would expect rates in the non-competitive category to be relatively higher, ceteris paribus, compared with rates in the competitive category. When class rates are excluded (we have already shown in Table 1 that only a small proportion of traffic moves under these rates and that costs are probably high on account of the small volume of traffic) the data indicate that the lowest average rate per ton-mile is found in the commodity non-competitive rate category. Care should, of course, be exercised in interpreting this result. Generally, commodity non-competitive rates are on commodities moving in bulk and thus the cost to the carrier is relatively low compared with costs for non-bulk shipments. An analysis of commodities moving under commodity non-competitive rates reveal two characteristics: a low value per ton and non-uniqueness. The latter means that the commodity has more than one production point and thus the output from more than a single point is competing in market areas.

The reason for the low rate per ton-mile for this type of traffic is that although the cross-elasticity of demand between modes for such commodities is generally low, the demand curve facing the carrier is relatively elastic with respect to rates. If the monopoly carrier raises rates, total revenue from this type of traffic would decline.

In most cases, competition from other transport modes is either present or potentially present. In estimating the demand for rail and truck transportation in the United States, Morton (1969) finds the price elasticity of demand for rail transportation to be very close to -1, with a cross-elasticity of demand between the two modes of 0.93.[5] In an analysis of transportation demand, a study by the Canadian Transport Commission (1975) estimates own-price elasticities for rail transportation demand for a selected group of commodities. Although the elasticity coefficiant tended to be low for some bulk commodities (those normally shipped under commodity non-competitive rates), the elasticity coefficient for an 'all' commodity group was equal to -1. These results, although partial in nature, imply competition between transport modes.

In Canada, the authority to regulate intraprovincial highway trucking rests with provincial governments. In some provinces, particularly Ontario and Quebec, the industry is highly regulated. From an economic viewpoint the regulation of this industry is extremely hard to defend. The industry is

5 Morton's data pertain to common carrier trucking and railroads.

characterized by low capital investment entry requirements, and the underlying production function does not reveal the presence of important scale economies (Warner, 1967). Meyer, in an article on competition, concluded that 'so-called economies of scale would appear to be equally available to small and large firms' (Meyer et al., 1959, 97).

Theory therefore suggests that the trucking industry is one where, in the absence of regulation, vigorous competition in levels of rates and service can be expected. The trucking industry in Canada has been a major supporter of regulation. The arguments typically advanced by the industry allege that deregulation would not be in the public interest, since it would lead to 'unsafe vehicles,' 'destructive competition,' 'monopoly,' 'poor service,' 'large number of bankruptcies leading to instability in the level of rates and number of carriers.' Joy (1964) analysed the effect of deregulation of highway trucking in Australia and found no evidence of 'destructive competition' or 'instability.' There is also little basis to suggest that in the absence of regulation, the industry would assume a monopolistic structure. The cost of entry is minimal and thus predatory pricing on the part of a large company would not be profitable. In the United Kingdom, where rate regulation is not practised for highway carriers and where entry into the industry is easy, the available evidence indicates no trend towards a monopoly situation (Gwilliam, 1964; Central Office of Information, 1976).

In Ontario, entry into for-hire trucking is controlled by the Ontario Highway Trucking Board (OHTB). To acquire a licence for a specific route the applicant must either purchase an existing carrier's licence or obtain one from the Board. The basic criterion for the granting or not granting of a licence is that of 'public necessity and convenience.' The Board publishes all requests for licences in the *Ontario Gazette*, together with the date of hearing for the application. At the present time a high proportion of all applications are opposed by existing carriers (Palmer, 1974).

The Board has no formal control over the level of rates. All rates must be filed with the Board, but the Board has no power to accept or reject rates set by carriers. Palmer, however, suggests that disagreements over rate levels are at the heart of licence application debates.

With respect to existing licences, a market operates similar to that reported by Friedman (1962) for New York City taxicab medallions. A carrier can sell his licence, subject to the approval of the OHTB. Palmer (1974) observes that in only a few cases is the transfer request refused. The transfer value of an existing licence will reflect the expected level of profit to be earned on the route. In brief, the cash value of the licence can be thought of as the discounted capitalized value of expected monopoly rents. It is, of course, difficult to ascertain the current market price of existing licences. Palmer suggests that on some routes the level was between $4,000 and $20,000. The price for a licence on a high-volume route with a limited number of carriers is probably greatly in excess of those figures.

If rates of return in the industry were normal, the value of an existing licence would be zero. The operation of the OHTB thus represents an institutionalized barrier to the optimal allocation of resources. Because of severe entry restrictions, highway rates can be expected to be above those which would prevail in the absence of such restrictions.

In separate studies, Sloss (1970), McLachlan (1972), and Palmer (1973) have attempted to measure the effect of rate regulation on highway rates. In all studies it was shown that rates in the regulated provinces were higher than in those where rates were not regulated. Using aggregate data, Palmer shows that rate regulation led to rates which were up to 2¢ higher per ton-mile in the regulated provinces than in the non-regulated provinces. In the specific case of Northern Ontario, a recent study (Ministry of Transportation and Communications, 1976) finds that the level of rates on specified routes is inversely related to the number of competing carriers. As the number of carriers increases, the level of rates decreases.

It is highly probable that some rail rates are set at a level higher than would result in the face of a competitive trucking industry. If trucking rates are higher than under competition, rail carriers can set agreed charge and commodity competitive rates to reflect this fact. If trucking rates were reduced, rail rates in the competitive category would also need to decline in order for rail carriers to preserve their share of the market.

Entry restriction and rate regulation in the highway trucking industry are thus seen as causes for both high trucking and rail rates on commodities for which the cross-elasticity of demand between the modes is large. Deregulation would therefore yield two important benefits: lower truck rates and lower rail rates on some commodities. In effect, increased competition in the highway industry will decrease the level of price discrimination practised by both modes.

6

Transportation costs and Northern Ontario economic development

In this chapter we seek to analyse the importance of transportation costs on the economic development of Northern Ontario. There are two main considerations: first, whether the existing structure of freight rates in Canada discriminates against producers located in Northern Ontario compared with producers located in other parts of Canada; second, whether the absolute level of transportation costs for producers located in Northern Ontario can be seen as a significant barrier to regional development.

With respect to the first consideration, the regression analysis conducted in chapter 4 clearly shows that rates for shipments originating in Northern Ontario destined for other parts of Canada are significantly lower than rates for shipments originating in other parts of Canada destined for Northern Ontario. This differential is mainly due to the nature of production in the regional economy. A large proportion of total regional output can be classified as raw or fabricated materials. Because of the high volume of such shipments and actual or potential competition between transport modes, a high percentage of regional output moves to market under agreed charge and commodity competitive rates, although the former dominates. As was shown earlier, the average rate per ton-mile for traffic moving under such rates is relatively low.

Rates on in-bound shipments are higher than the rates on out-bound movements for two reasons. First, a high proportion of goods moving into the region are manufactured goods or finished commodities. We have already shown that rates on such goods are considerably higher than rates on crude or semi-finished commodities. Second, most items moving into the region are in insufficient volume to obtain the benefit of agreed charge rates.

Our analysis of rates suggests that for the rail mode rates on the major outputs of the regional economy moving from major production centres are not statistically significantly different from rates on traffic originating in other regions moving in similar volumes similar distances. To provide more detailed information, regression analysis was applied to agreed charge rate cases with respect to originating region and commodity type. It is to be noted that the average rate per ton-mile for given commodities moving under agreed charge rates was approximately 15 per cent lower than the rates for the same commodities moving under commodity competitive rates.

The average rate per ton-mile for all rail traffic originating in Northern Ontario subject to agreed charge rates was 3.3 cents. Rates for traffic originating in the Northwestern portion of the region were lower than those for traffic originating in the Northeastern portion, primarily because distance transported was higher for the former than the latter.

Commodities in the woods product category originating in Northern Ontario and moving under agreed charge rates had an average rate per ton mile of 3.34 cents for an average distance of 948 miles and average weight of 87,050 lbs. In comparison, the average rate per ton-mile for similar traffic subject to agreed charge rates originating in other parts of Ontario and Quebec was 3.55 cents for an average distance of 616 miles and average weight of 100,865 lbs.

In order to provide more information, an examination of residuals was undertaken. For traffic terminating and originating in each region, residuals were plotted against distance, weight, and value. With respect to rail traffic, the plot of residuals against distance revealed that for shipments terminating in Northern Ontario and the Maritimes the residuals generally had positive values (that is, they were above the regression line). For traffic terminating in other regions, especially the East, they tended to have negative values (that is, they fell into the hyperbolic bag below the regression line). For rail traffic originating in Northern Ontario, the residuals were mainly negative and fell into the hyperbolic bag. With regard to the weight variable the pattern of residuals across regions was not significantly different. The plot of residuals against value revealed that for shipments originating in Quebec and the non-northern part of Ontario, the residuals were consistently above the regression line. This could be caused by the fact that a high proportion of high-value shipments originate in this area, combined with the fact that rail carriers are able to discriminate in rates with respect to value.

For highway movements the plot of residuals against distance revealed the presence of a hyperbolic bag beneath the regression line. Amongst originating traffic more residuals fell above the regression line for shipments originating in Ontario (excluding the northern portion) and Quebec than for shipments originating in other regions. For Northern Ontario approximately 65 per cent of the residuals fell into the bag. For terminating traffic a higher proportion of the residuals for Northern Ontario fell above the line than for traffic terminating in other parts of Ontario and Quebec. In the case of weight, the residuals were slightly higher for both terminating and originating Northern Ontario traffic than for other regions. The plot of residuals against value revealed no major differences across regions, except that among shipments terminating in Quebec and the non-northern portion of Ontario the residuals were slightly lower than in other regions. An analysis of the over-all residuals was generally inconclusive, except that in the case of rail shipments the residuals for traffic terminating in Northern Ontario were slightly higher than for shipments terminating in other regions.

One of the major problems with transportation costs is not immediately apparent from the analysis. Small-volume shippers located in Northern Ontario, and especially in the non-major centres, face relatively higher transportation costs than large volume shippers. Such shippers are usually not able to take advantage of the competitive rates offered by rail and highway carriers, so that their goods must be shipped either under the class rate structure or by non-for-hire truck transportation. Although rail class rates are not significantly different from region to region (except for the reduction given to traffic originating in the select territory), they are very much higher than rates for the same commodity moving under agreed charge or competitive rate forms. For example, carload traffic moving under class 55 yields the carrier an average revenue per ton-mile of 12.77 cents for a distance of 811 miles, 14.23 cents for a distance of 551 miles, and 25.32 cents for a distance of 188 miles. The rate on agreed charge traffic of this nature is between one-third and one-half the class rate.

The agreed charge and competitive rate structures clearly reduce the locational disadvantages of producers located in Northern Ontario. If such rates were not available, a regional producer shipping output to the major markets of Southern Ontario and Quebec would be at a great disadvantage in transport costs compared to a producer located much nearer the market area. Thus the non-availability of competitive rate forms works against some small-volume shippers locating in the region, unless there are advantages to offset the high transportation costs.

The high level of rates on in-bound movements is detrimental to the region's ability to diversify from its existing narrow export base. One of the major problems in this connection is that a wide variety of inputs needed by a typical secondary manufacturer are not produced within the region and thus must be shipped in from distant centres. Since the volume of such shipments between specific origin-destination pairs is likely to be small, shippers cannot obtain the benefit of competitive rate forms. To an extent there is a vicious circle here: in order for rates on in-bound shipments to fall, the volume of such shipments must rise, but volume can only rise if the region expands. At the margin, the high level of rates inhibit regional expansion of the type required to increase the flow of many production inputs. Thus to some degree the situation is self-perpetuating.

It has been noted elsewhere that highway rates in Ontario are among the highest in Canada. In chapter 5 it was postulated that the major reason for this can be traced to the fact that the Ontario Highway Trucking Board has a restrictive entry policy. A study by the Ontario Ministry of Transportation and Communications found that one of the reasons for high truck rates on certain routes was the lack of intramodel competition.[1] The absence of vigorous competition in the Ontario trucking industry has far-reaching consequences for the over-all level of transportation costs. Since rail carriers actively pursue a value-for-service pricing principle, rail rates will be higher in the absence of competition in the trucking industry. Restrictions on the entry of carriers into the Ontario highway trucking industry thus can be seen as one of the causes for high freight rates — both road and rail — in the province. Unfortunately we were not able to examine the number and type of licences issued to carriers on specified routes in Ontario, and in consequence could not determine whether the high level of highway rates on commodities in-bound to the region was a direct result of a lack of competition. From a theoretical viewpoint, however, this appears highly probable.

With the existing major outputs of the regional economy, the absence of vigorous competition probably has little impact on the ability of regional producers to compete effectively in major markets. Because of the high volume of specific commodity traffic flows originating in the major centres of the region, major producers are able to obtain freight rates that are not significantly different from those available to similar producers located in other regions. The transportation costs of shipping output to markets are thus not large enough to negate the region's natural advantages in access to raw material inputs such as wood and mineral ores.

Our analysis indicates, however, that the existing structure of freight rates discourages the establishment of secondary manufacturing plants within the region. The reliance by carriers on a value-for-service pricing principle has led to high freight rates on many production inputs that must be transported into the

1 For the published portion of the study, see Ministry of Transportation and Communications (1976).

region and to high rates on shipping secondary manufactured products to market. This, coupled with the large distances involved, implies that many Northern Ontario centres are relatively unattractive as potential locations for secondary manufacturing producers.

Some of the disadvantages of high freight rates in this connection can be eliminated by policies designed to foster rather than inhibit competition in the Ontario highway trucking industry. The promotion of strong competition within the highway trucking industry will lower many highway trucking rates. In addition, it would have the added benefit of restricting the ability of rail carriers to indulge in price discrimination. Given the type of commodities best suited to truck transportation (non-bulk higher-value commodities), we would expect freight rates to, from, and within Northern Ontario to decline on precisely those commodities whose rates are considered unduly high.

The promotion of vigorous competition in the trucking industry is, from a practical viewpoint, easier to achieve than the enactment of a transportation subsidy designed to eliminate some of the transportation cost disadvantages of a Northern Ontario location. We have already shown in chapter 5 that a subsidy by itself will not necessarily lead to benefits to shippers commensurate with the size of the subsidy if transportation rates are set in the absence of a competitive environment. In the case of Northern Ontario, transportation rates on most inputs and outputs are not formed in a competitive climate. Thus the benefits of a subsidy will not all accrue to the intended beneficiaries.

The results and analysis contained in this study strongly suggest that one of the barriers to the region's ability to diversify from its present narrow resource-oriented base is the presence of high freight rates. This barrier can be significantly reduced by policies designed to allow vigorous competition in the Ontario trucking industry.

Description of data and sources

The transportation rates used in this study were in force during the period May to September 1975. Rate adjustments, both in rate levels and the application of rates, do not occur simultaneously for all rates. To avoid an obvious source of bias, rates due to expire before 1 August were not included in the data base. Similarly, rates due to come into operation after 1 August were also excluded from the data base.

It should be noted that the rate levels obtained in this study cannot be updated from year to year merely by applying the national average percentage rate changes. Most rate changes are selective, and the percentage increase (in some cases decrease) varies by commodity and route. Moreover, one type of rate may be substituted for another; for example, it appears that rail carriers are replacing some of the agreed charge rates on lumber shipments originating in the West with commodity competitive rates.

RAIL RATES

The data base for rail is composed largely of agreed charge and commodity rates, obtained from the Canadian Freight Association and the two major rail carriers. All rates are published and open to inspection under the authority of the Railway Act. Commodity and agreed charge rates are normally quoted in cents per 100 lbs for specific origin-destination pairs. All rates were converted to cents per ton and distance was computed for each case. Rates are usually quoted for various minimum weight categories. As an example, CFA Tariff 500 shows that for item 13480 (iron or steel articles in carloads moving from Montreal to

Thunder Bay under commodity rates), the rate per 100 lb is 207 cents for a minimum shipment weight of 40,000 lb. This drops to 143 cents per 100 lb for a minimum shipment weight of 140,000 lb.

In the case of agreed charge rates, the carriers and shippers subject to the rate are stated, as are restrictions on the application of the rate. For example, agreed charge 2958 between Anglo-Canadian Pulp and Paper Mills Ltd and CP and CN applies to the movement of pulpboard between Quebec and Toronto with a conditional volume of 90 per cent. This means that 90 per cent of 'the said traffic' (the pulpboard) must be shipped under the rate. If the shipper defaults on this agreement the carriers have the right to damages, defined in this case as the difference between the agreed charge rate and the regular tariff rate on all goods actually shipped *plus* 10 per cent of the agreed charge rate. Under this agreement the carriers have the right to inspect the shipper's shipping books. In other instances a condition is imposed on the rate and flow of shipments. For example, agreed charge 433-J, in operation between 3 January and 15 April 1975 for the movement of export grain between Armstrong/Thunder Bay and Montreal/Quebec, was predicated on rail carriers handling a volume of between 5 and 8 million bushels, the carriers receiving an equal volume with 2 per cent tolerance.

For the construction of back-haul statistics, it was assumed that the interprovincial flows for 1975 were proportional to those of 1973. This assumption was necessary because the latest publication of the Commodity Flow Analysis (Canadian Transport Commission, 1974) is for the 1973 year. As stated in chapter 3, grain movements were eliminated. As an example of the calculation involved, consider the case of movements between the Maritimes and Quebec and Ontario. According to the commodity flow data, 1,308,000 tons originated in the Maritimes and moved to Quebec, and 980,000 tons moved from the Maritimes to Ontario. The reverse movements were 1,770,000 and 2,517,000. Thus the probability of a back-haul for Maritime cars moving to Quebec and Ontario was 100 per cent, whereas for traffic moving from Quebec to the Maritimes the back-haul probability was only 73.9 per cent. The corresponding figure for Ontario to the Maritimes was 38.9 per cent. When grain movements are eliminated from consideration, the difference in traffic flow directions for all parts of Canada is small, with the obvious exception of the Maritimes.

In order to provide a partial check on the validity of the data base, regression analysis was applied to data given in the 1973 waybill analysis. Figures for volume, length of haul, weight, and rate per ton-mile were extracted for all commodities other than those classified as food or feed. The movement of traffic in the two latter classes was excluded primarily because a large proportion of the traffic was covered by statutory rates.

The waybill data pertain to an overaged set of trip characteristics for sample movements in approximately 310 separate commodity categories. Data were assembled for four distinct hauls: East-to-West, West-to-East, East-to-East, and West-to-West. Movements to, from, and within the Maritimes were excluded because observations were insufficient to yield adequate degrees of freedom. If a commodity gave rise to an East-to-West and West-to-East haul, it was included in the sample. However, a one-way movement only was not included. A similar criterion was applied to data on intra-region movements. Any obviously 'odd' movement was excluded. These fell into two categories: those where rates were inordinately high (57.84 cents per ton-mile for a nineteen-mile haul as an example) and those where rates were so low as to lead us to believe that rates were based on using non-carrier-supplied cars.

In the case of East-to-West rates, average distance was 2003 miles, weight was 35.75 tons, and the average rate per ton-mile was 3.1116 cents. For West-to-East traffic, the average distance was 1947 miles, weight was 41.9 tons, and the average rate per ton-mile 2.20 cents. The regression analysis revealed that the best fit was obtained with distance and weight coefficients specified in inverse form. Coefficients for both of these variables were statistically significant and of the postulated sign.

As can be seen, the results for inter-regional shipments between the two regions are in accordance with the regression results obtained in chapter 4. The large difference in rate levels between East-to-West and West-to-East movements cannot be ascribed to the weight differential.

With respect to intra-regional shipments, East-to-East rates were higher than West-to-West rates. The data were split into three separate groups: inedible crude materials, inedible fabricated materials, and inedible end products. In all three cases the average length of the West-to-West haul and the average weight of shipments was higher than for East-to-East movements.

HIGHWAY RATES

Data for highway rates were assembled from information provided by provincial highway tariff bureaus and from individual carriers. Highway rates were less uniform than rail rates. In many provinces, Ontario for example, carriers are not compelled to file identical rates or conform to rates set by the regulatory body. The operation of rate bureaus does, however, tend to limit rate diversity.

VALUE OF SHIPMENTS

The data for commodity values were obtained from Statistics Canada published sources, basically from the annual Census of Manufacturing. In most cases the latest figures available were those for 1972. The data on values were therefore converted to mid-1975 figures by the use of price indexes.

COMMODITY CODES

231-239 Crude wood materials
241-246 Textile and related products
251-259 Metal ores, metal in ores, concentrates, and scrap
261-263 Coal, crude petroleum, and related crude products
271-279 Crude non-metallic minerals (except coal and petroleum)
321-325 Rubber and plastic fabricated materials
331-339 Wood fabricated materials
341-342 Pulp
351-359 Paper and paperboard
361-389 Textile fabricated materials
400-429 Chemicals and related products
431-439 Petroleum and coal products
441-449 Iron, steel, and alloys
451-459 Non-ferrous metals
461-469 Metal-fabricated basic products
501-551 Machinery
671-673 Plumbing equipment and fittings
681-689 Electric lighting, distribution, and control equipment
741-748 Furniture and fixtures
891-899 Printed matter
941-947 Miscellaneous end-products
961-969 Remaining end-products classified by materials

TABLE A1

Sample rail cases for traffic originating in the East

Case	Commodity	Distance	Rate	Rate/Value
1	444	2730	1.84	7.57
2	444	390	5.02	2.95
3	231	85	4.23	10.00
4	444	658	2.37	5.57
5	337	479	2.96	3.96
6	336	190	5.47	4.00
7	336	618	2.29	5.46
8	336	820	1.82	5.77
9	354	565	3.46	4.79
10	354	815	3.41	6.79
11	354	430	3.11	3.27
12	335	735	1.94	10.09
13	338	1619	2.08	20.02
14	338	376	2.07	4.67
15	445	505	3.08	5.15
16	354	1180	4.20	7.98
17	432	104	2.69	0.75
18	461	2875	3.36	5.37
19	461	2695	3.59	5.37
20	339	1509	2.21	10.07
21	339	1043	2.89	9.11
22	351	2862	3.31	15.07
23	351	245	5.38	4.51
24	351	735	3.07	10.39
25	353	1230	5.25	6.99
26	353	2054	4.67	10.39
27	338	1873	3.43	38.52
28	338	2041	4.23	51.60
29	339	2862	2.55	32.90
30	353	750	4.26	3.46
31	353	591	5.21	3.33
32	442	1460	3.04	32.10
33	442	731	2.65	16.00
34	236	170	4.23	10.40
35	444	846	4.51	5.74
36	444	731	2.95	3.25
37	337	1758	4.91	24.80
38	337	493	8.31	11.84
39	337	1937	4.83	27.00
40	337	1049	5.64	17.10

TABLE A2

Sample rail cases for traffic originating in the West

Case	Commodity	Distance	Rate	Rate/Value
1	356	824	5.097	13.70
2	356	848	4.953	13.70
3	356	758	5.541	13.70
4	356	657	6.393	13.70
5	354	2870	1.895	7.54
6	354	2687	2.025	7.54
7	354	2695	2.019	7.54
8	255	2323	1.343	0.81
9	255	2088	1.494	0.81
10	335	720	1.889	9.92
11	338	1779	1.619	17.39
12	333	1931	1.937	28.18
13	333	1429	2.477	27.18
14	333	1656	2.138	27.18
15	333	2154	1.736	28.71
16	333	1713	2.067	27.18
17	333	1441	2.457	27.18
18	333	1934	1.830	27.18
19	255	2971	1.299	0.91
20	255	2271	1.488	0.91
21	341	1080	1.667	6.82
22	351	1243	2.011	3.97
23	351	1292	1.935	3.97
24	351	1404	1.892	4.22
25	351	1553	1.958	4.83
26	444	1440	1.569	3.40
27	444	1740	1.448	3.79
28	444	1818	2.343	6.40
29	356	1893	3.656	4.70
30	356	1688	1.765	20.50
31	356	927	1.942	12.39
32	356	880	2.024	12.25
33	356	630	2.476	10.73
34	356	811	2.000	11.70
35	354	1410	1.645	5.89
36	354	2707	1.751	12.03
37	331	2486	1.327	15.44
38	331	2042	1.469	14.07
39	351	2096	2.643	7.03
40	356	773	2.717	7.32

TABLE A3

Sample rail cases for traffic originating in the select territory

Case	Commodity	Distance	Rate	Rate/Value
1	964	2973	3.653	23.52
2	964	2997	3.624	23.52
3	964	3364	3.906	28.44
4	964	3514	3.802	28.92
5	964	2507	3.742	20.30
6	964	3629	2.717	21.34
7	964	1740	3.230	12.16
8	964	3728	3.171	25.58
9	339	285	6.175	4.40
10	339	290	6.069	4.42
11	339	285	5.440	6.95
12	339	922	2.213	9.20
13	339	1017	2.163	9.93
14	339	140	5.429	3.43
15	339	537	2.086	5.05
16	339	240	3.417	3.70
17	339	877	2.098	8.30
18	231	2774	2.567	80.01
19	231	2804	2.539	79.91
20	231	3415	2.331	82.25
21	231	1950	2.882	62.30
22	446	3991	3.348	48.06
23	446	3695	3.616	48.06
24	446	3574	3.917	50.37
25	446	3574	1.399	17.99
26	446	2933	2.203	23.24
27	338	1950	4.349	44.95
28	338	1825	4.647	44.95
29	333	1075	3.758	31.90
30	333	700	4.029	22.80

TABLE A4

Sample cases for highway traffic originating in the East

Case	Commodity	Distance	Rate	Rate/Value
1	331	380	2.779	4.95
2	331	495	2.667	6.38
3	331	300	3.520	4.95
4	331	190	5.095	4.54
5	331	605	2.182	6.19
6	331	600	2.200	6.19
7	252	60	9.333	0.64
8	252	40	14.000	0.64
9	252	260	10.233	3.03
10	252	435	10.989	5.45
11	339	597	3.250	6.82
12	339	558	3.477	6.82
13	945	445	4.404	1.49
14	945	212	9.245	1.46
15	433	285	6.246	3.12
16	451	200	8.000	1.60
17	494	60	7.000	3.28
18	339	650	3.785	12.53
19	339	743	3.445	13.03
20	339	806	3.325	13.65
21	354	2937	5.032	20.47
22	354	2372	5.514	18.12
23	354	1215	3.654	11.28
24	351	2293	3.681	14.82
25	351	2277	3.654	14.61
26	337	435	4.322	5.24
27	339	585	2.906	5.97
28	338	940	4.362	16.30
29	461	1463	2.707	13.75
30	469	2398	3.536	11.10

TABLE A5

Sample highway cases for traffic originating in the West

Case	Commodity	Distance	Rate	Rate/Value
1	351	1418	2.375	5.33
2	351	1255	2.422	4.82
3	351	900	2.289	3.48
4	448	2293	2.032	14.62
5	448	1818	2.079	11.86
6	448	1463	2.105	9.66
7	331	1255	1.880	15.17
8	452	2710	2.177	2.30
9	452	2850	2.863	3.18
10	588	2293	3.515	5.28
11	588	2306	3.495	5.33
12	588	1463	2.939	2.82
13	353	2449	3.332	2.72
14	353	1863	2.802	1.80
15	353	2019	3.210	2.20
16	461	1343	2.547	11.95
17	461	2293	1.971	15.79
18	351	1348	2.641	5.65
19	351	1415	2.516	5.65
20	341	700	3.300	9.00

TABLE A6

Sample cases for highway traffic originating in the select territory

Case	Commodity	Distance	Rate	Rate/Value
1	339	650	2.923	6.70
2	339	500	3.800	6.70
3	339	520	3.423	8.16
4	339	700	3.086	9.00
5	331	700	6.829	8.36
6	444	534	2.509	4.49
7	444	384	3.333	4.29
8	444	476	3.193	5.09
9	461	510	3.805	6.77
10	461	630	3.810	8.38
11	461	500	3.640	6.32
12	461	380	4.632	6.14
13	433	620	6.387	5.99
14	433	570	3.719	3.60
15	433	429	4.196	3.10
16	339	575	3.409	8.90
17	339	680	4.382	10.56
18	331	355	4.169	—
19	464	207	6.820	1.00
20	464	433	6.200	1.90

TABLE A7

Regression results for rail by commodity breakdown

Commodity	R/D	a	b1	b2	F	R²
230-240	2.89	3.29	230	−108926*	20.9	0.57
250-260	1.79	−78	479*	43102	1385	0.99
330-340	3.63	1.00	907*	166568	25143	0.98
350-360	3.92	2.68	123	51210	17.8	0.15
440-450	4.31	3.43	460*	197731*	150	0.84
460-470	2.87	0.68	800*	33229*	21.7	0.91

NOTE: R/D is the average rate per ton-mile in cents, a is a constant, b1 is the coefficient for 1/Distance, and b2 is the coefficient for 1/Weight. Coefficients statistically significant at the 95 per cent level are marked with an asterisk.

TABLE A8

Regression results for highway by commodity breakdown

Commodity	R/D	a	b1	b2	F	R²
250-260	8.53	−2.18	230*	210011*	89.7	0.82
330-340	3.23	2.61	661*	−19709	20.1	0.47
350-360	3.68	3.75	−640	1950*	47	0.69
430-440	5.29	5.51	94.4*	−1021*	6.5	0.67
440-450	3.98	.35	860*	48720*	58	0.95
450-460	8.82	−.82	674*	31771*	292	0.90
460-470	4.57	2.24	671	30550*	256	0.90
470-480	4.23	2.37	777*	20383*	28	0.82

NOTE: see note to Table A7.

TABLE A9

Regression results for rail by region

Origin-Destination	R/D	a	$b1$	$b2$	$b3$	AC	F	R^2
Select-East	2.32	2.91	101	19773*	−169.0	0	50	0.95
East-Select	3.31	2.89	1610*	21963*	−427.0*	−0.03	292	0.92
East-West	3.55	2.50	420*	96317*	−8.3	−1.76*	64	0.59
East-East	3.68	0.35	943*	337672*	−6.4	0.49	300	0.74
West-East	2.03	0.79	379*	62520*	16.9*	0.17	15	0.50
West-West	3.5	2.96	149*	57884*	−3.5*	0	298	0.98
All-Select	3.46	0.88	585*	68132*	−52.0*	0.71	37	0.74
Select-All	3.17	2.09	559*	60686*	−14.0	−1.26*	25	0.51
Toronto-All	3.60	2.99	679*	68056*	−122.0*	−1.15*	34	0.64
All-Toronto	2.65	3.46	903*	80439*	17.0*	0	94	0.82
North Ont-All	3.70	1.76	870*	138418*	−14.2*	−1.96*	964	0.88
All-North Ont.	7.07	−0.27	899*	141077*	−41.0*	−0.06	2255	0.99
All-Winnipeg	4.12	0.96	2080*	103140*	2.36*	1.65*	1478	0.46
Select-West	3.03	1.33	90	106220*	3.48	−2.06*	23	0.65

NOTE: R/D is the average rate per ton-mile in cents, a is a constant, $b1$ is the coefficient for 1/Distance, $b2$ is the coefficient for 1/Weight, $b3$ is the coefficient for 1/Value, and AC is a dummy variable for agreed charges. Coefficients statistically significant at the 95 per cent level are marked with an asterisk.

TABLE A10

Regression results for highway by region

Origin-Destination	R/D	a	$b1$	$b2$	$b3$	F	R^2
Select-East	4.16	7.8	−314	−3935	−54.6	25	0.64
East-Select	6.22	3.33	460*	7242*	−18.59	8	0.63
East-West	3.76	2.97	1162*	2037*	−1.08	52	0.43
East-East	6.32	1.51	390*	10958*	−205*	313	0.75
West-East	2.77	1.65	1507	25128	−189	39	0.65
All-Select	6.19	0.85	395	77116	13.69	8	0.35
Select-All	4.17	7.56	−110.3	−4934	−556*	25	0.64
Toronto-All	8.2	−0.05	360*	190005	102*	158	0.73
All-Toronto	8.67	−1.6	453*	233500	624*	82	0.84
North Ont-All	3.7	3.03	639*	5446	−124*	42	0.48
All-North Ont.	5.06	1.95	715*	69543	−160*	38	0.55
All-Winnipeg	3.6	2.25	1708	2510	2.2	5.6	0.34

NOTE: see note to Table A9.

The impact of statutory grain rates on the rate structure

In chapter 2 it was shown that 25 to 27 per cent of total rail ton-miles were performed under rates which were 3 cents per 100 lb below the rates prevailing in 1899. The statutory grain rates yield the rail carriers an average revenue per ton-mile of approximately 0.48 cents. In contrast, the lowest non-statutory rates available in 1975 for a distance of 900 to 1,000 miles (chosen to approximate the average distance grain is shipped under the statutory rates) were approximately 1.03 cents a ton-mile.

The question arises whether or not the statutory grain rates lead to an upward pressure on non-statutory rates through a process of cross-subsidization. The answer depends on whether the statutory rates are set sufficiently high to cover costs and, if not, whether any loss is passed on to other traffic in the form of higher rates or results in a lower rate of return on investment.

Major Canadian rail carriers have frequently advanced the opinion that the statutory grain rates are not compensatory. The Canadian Pacific Railroad argued before the 1951 Royal Commission on Transportation that, based on 1948 grain movements and costs, they suffered a shortfall on 'out-of-pocket' expenses of between $13.8 million and $16.9 million (Royal Commission on Transportation, 1951, 224). The 1961 Royal Commission on Transportation concluded that the statutory rates failed to cover variable cost by $6 million and revenues were below fully allocated cost by $16.3 million (Royal Commission on Transportation, 1961, Vol. 1, 82). A 1975 study by the CPR claimed a total loss on the 1973 movement of grain by the carrier of $51.9 million (CP Rail, 1975). This figure treats the subsidy paid for uneconomic branch lines as grain related revenue.

The critical problem in analysing the effect of statutory grain rates concerns the way costs are to be measured and whether or not rates should be based on marginal cost. In a competitive market, economic theory leads to the proposition that, in the long run, prices set equal to marginal cost will secure an optimal allocation of resources. The application of this principle to railroad pricing has been discussed in detail by Baumol et al. (1962, 1-10), Meyer et al. (1959), and Roberts (1965). Essentially, a problem is caused by the length of time in which some items of railroad capital are 'fixed' and the question of joint and common costs. Roberts, a proponent of marginal cost pricing, states about the former that 'the "theoretically pure" long run (contemplating complete variability) is, in the railroad case, an abstraction completely devoid of practical significance. As is well known, large elements of rail plant are not re-produced over very long time periods ... Substantial elements of rail cost remain fixed over any period relevant for either management or regulatory decisions' (1965, 7).

In addressing the question of joint and common costs, Meyer et al. find that such costs are a 'substantial sum' which cannot be allocated to any specific traffic, except on the basis of demand. Because of the presence of such costs, 'any realistic measure of "long-run" marginal costs will not exhaust all costs to ensure against bankruptcy' (ibid.).

For statutory grain rates, it is empirically difficult to determine the long-run marginal cost of moving grain. To begin with, the following points should be noted. First, if rates are insufficient to cover long-run marginal cost they lead to a compulsory misallocation of resources since resources are provided for which the price of the service is less than marginal cost. Second, if the rates do not allow a portion of the unallocatable costs to be covered, such costs will have to be borne by other traffic.

The analysis of grain transport losses in the 1975 CPR study is not particularly helpful. The costing techniques employed imply that losses have been computed on the basis of fully allocated cost pricing. This of course will lead to an overstatement of the economic level of losses if excess capacity exists. It implies, for example, that a 'normal rate of return' is to be earned on fixed assets, which are the result of past investment decisions. This is inappropriate where excess capacity exists. In a competitive market, if price is above the level of marginal cost but below the level of average total cost, the service would be provided in the short run. As capital becomes worn out, it would not be replaced.

Statistically, the existing published information is totally inadequate to allow for an accurate derivation of long-run marginal cost for grain transportation. The analysis is further complicated by the fact that there is not a measureable demand curve for grain transportation by rail. The transport seller's price is set, and all grain offered to the rail carriers at that price must be carried.

In the absence of detailed cost information, the best that can be hoped for is a very rough estimate of the adequacy or inadequacy of the grain rates. For the period January to April 1975, an agreed charge was in force on export grain moving from Thunder Bay to Montreal and Quebec. This agreed charge was very restrictive in that, for wheat, the minimum weight was 120,000 lb per boxcar and applicable on trains between seventy-two and ninety-three cars. In addition, the agreed charge was applicable only during the railroads' off-peak periods. The rate per ton-mile for wheat was 1.0312 cents to Montreal, and 0.8983 cents to Quebec.

It can be argued that the above rate, which does not include terminal charges or loading and unloading, is probably relatively close to off-peak marginal cost for traffic of this type. Long-run marginal cost, especially during peak periods, can be hypothesized to be in excess of this level. If it is assumed, however, that 0.8983 cents a ton-mile is equal to marginal cost, then the existing statutory rate is considerably below this level. A marginal cost per ton-mile of 0.8983 cents would imply that for 1975 – assuming that grain traffic remained at the 1973 level – revenue from the statutory grain rates was below summed marginal cost by approximately $100 million. This figure refers to the loss after the branch-line subsidy has been allowed for, but does not include any allowance for government ownership of some grain cars.

Assuming a loss of considerable magnitude is caused by the level of the statutory grain rates, it is probable that some, if not all, of the loss is met by cross-subsidization. In brief, the loss on statutory grain transportation may well be responsible for higher rates on other commodities than would have been the case in the absence of such losses. The submission by the CPR to the 1951 Royal Commission on Transportation in effect argued this position (Royal Commission on Transportation, 1951, 252). The ability of a rail carrier to pass on this loss to other traffic is determined by the rate elasticity of the various demand curves facing him. In the case where the rail carrier faces effective competition from other transport modes, or where the commodity has a relatively elastic demand curve for transportation services by virtue of its low value per ton, we would expect the quantity of rail transport demanded to be relatively sensitive to railroad rates. In this situation we would expect a large portion of the loss to be borne by rail traffic which displays a relatively inelastic demand for railroad transportation with respect to rail rates.

Wilson and Darby (1968, 62) argue that the statutory grain rates and competition from other modes have caused the 'incidence of freight rate increases to fall more heavily upon a smaller range of commodities.' Essentially, they support the hypothesis that since low-value commodities cannot bear large rate increases without a significant drop in market demand, and since the railroads face severe competition from highway carriers for a large proportion of high-value commodities, rate increases have tended to be borne to a large extent by a small range of shipments. They conclude that statutory rates and competition 'both operate in the same direction, viz they preclude adoption of value-of-service pricing over a wide range of traffic thereby inducing a more vigorous adoption of value-of-service pricing on remaining traffic.' To the extent traffic of this type moves into and out of Northern Ontario, the statutory grain rates imply at the margin a reduction in the volume of such traffic.

Over time it is highly probable that the statutory grain rates will lead to increasing losses since costs increase with the level of inflation, but revenues are pegged by statute. The loss is directly related to volume: as volume increases, the loss also increases. If rail rates are at present set on all routes and commodities so as to maximize profit, greater cross-subsidization via more efficient price discrimination will not be possible because the most efficient form of price discrimination is already being practised. If and when this position is arrived at, the losses from statutory grain traffic will exert a downward pressure on the rate of return which cannot be compensated for by raising rates on other traffic. In the long run, this would imply a decrease in the rate of return to capital and, in a competitive market, a reduction in railroad capital investment.

References

Anderson, F.J. (1976a) 'The effects of remoteness on size in regional wage determination.' *Regional Studies* 10, 223-31
- (1976b) 'Demand conditions and supply constraints in regional economic growth.' *Journal of Regional Science* 16, 213-24
Anderson, F.J. and N.C. Bonsor (1974) 'Pricing and valuation of transport facilities in the presence of congestion.' *Economica* 41, 424-31
Archibald, G.C. (1972) 'On regional economic policy in the United Kingdom.' In M. Peston and B. Corry, eds, *Essays in Honour of Lord Robbins* (London: Weidenfeld and Nicolson)
Atlantic Region Freight Assistance Act, 17-18 Elizabeth II, chap. 52
Baumol, William J. et al. (1962) 'The role of cost in the minimum pricing of railroad services.' *Journal of Business* 35, 1-10
Bonsor, N.C. (1974) 'An optimal pricing strategy for scheduled air carriers over the North Atlantic.' *Logistics and Transportation Review* 10, 227-39.
Borts, G.H. (1954) 'Increasing returns in the railway industry.' *Journal of Political Economy* 62, 316-33
- (1960) 'The estimation of rail cost functions.' *Econometrica* 28, 108-31
Borts, G.H. and J.L. Stein (1964) 'Economic growth in a free market.' (New York: Columbia University Press)
CP Rail (1975) 'Analysis of grain transportation 1975.' (Montreal)
Canadian Transport Commission (1970) *Research Base for the Development of National Container Policy, Phase 1* (Ottawa)
- (1973) *Major Centre Traffic Flow 1971* (Ottawa)
- (1974) *1973 Waybill Analysis* (Ottawa)

- (1974) *Commodity Flow Analysis* (Ottawa)
- (1975) *Report on Transport Demand Forecasting Program: Phase One* (Ottawa)

Central Office of Information (1976) *Inland Transport in Britain* (London)

Currie, A.W. (1967) *Canadian Transportation Economics* (Toronto: University of Toronto Press)

Darling, H.J. (1974) *The Structure of Railroad Subsidies in Canada* (Toronto: York University Transport Centre)

- (1975) *An Historical Review of Direct Transport Subsidies in Canada* (Ottawa: Canadian Transport Commission)

Doganis, R. (1973) 'Air transportation — international regulation.' *Journal of Transport Economics and Policy* 7, 109-33

Draper, N.R. and H. Smith (1966) *Applied Regression Analysis* (New York: John Wiley and Sons)

Economist Intelligence Unit (1967) *Atlantic Provinces Transportation Study* (London)

Fair, M.L. and E.W. Williams (1975) *Economics of Transportation and Logistics* (Dallas: Business Publications)

Feltham, I.R. (1974) 'Transport regulation in Canada.' In K.W. Studnicki-Gizbert, ed., *Issues in Canadian Transport Policy* (Toronto: Macmillan of Canada)

Friedman, M. (1962) *Price Theory: A Provisional Text* (Chicago: Aldine)

George, R.E. (1970) *A Leader and A Laggard: Manufacturing Industry in Nova Scotia, Quebec and Ontario* (Toronto: University of Toronto Press)

Glazebrook, G.P. de T. (1938) *A History of Transportation in Canada* (Toronto: McClelland and Stewart)

Globe and Mail (1976) 'CN willing to switch equipment to Sultran,' 12 Feb., B14 (Toronto)

Government of Canada (1975) House of Commons *Debates* (Ottawa)

Griliches, Z. (1972) 'Cost allocation in railroad legislation.' *Bell Journal of Economics and Management Science* 3, 26-41

Guthrie, J.A. (1955) 'Economics of state and regional development.' *Regional Science Association Papers and Proceedings* 1, J1-J10

Gwilliam, K.M. (1964) *Transport and Public Policy* (London: George Allen and Unwin)

Haritos, Z. (1975) 'Transport costs and revenue in Canada.' *Journal of Transport Economics and Policy* 9, 16-32

Isaard, W. (1956) *Location and Space Economy* (Cambridge, Mass.: MIT Press)

Joy, Stewart (1964) *Unregulated Road Haulage: The Australian Experience.* Oxford Economic Papers, NS 16

Keeler, T. (1972) 'Airline regulation.' *Bell Journal of Economics and Management Science* 3, 399-424

Maritimes Freight Rates Act, 17 George V, 1927, Chap. 44

McLachlan, D.L. (1972) 'Canadian trucking regulation.' *Logistics and Transportation Review* 8, 59-81

Meyer, J.R., M.J. Peck, J. Stenason, and C. Zwick (1959) *The Economics of Competition in the Transportation Industries* (Cambridge, Mass.: Harvard University Press)

Meyer, J.R. and M. Wohl (1970) 'Alternative pricing strategies.' In J.R. Meyer, ed., *Techniques of Transport Planning* (Washington DC: The Brookings Institution)

Ministry of Transportation and Communications (1976) *An Investigation of Freight Rates and Related Problems: Northern Ontario* (Toronto)

Mohring, H. (1974) 'Transportation subsidies and the economic development of the Atlantic Provinces.' In K.J. Studnicki-Gizbert, ed., *Issues in Canadian Transport Policy* (Toronto: Macmillan of Canada)

Moore, T.G. (1975) 'Deregulating surface freight transportation.' In A. Phillips, ed., *Promoting Competition in Regulated Markets* (Washington DC: The Brookings Institution)

Morton, A.L. (1969) 'A statistical sketch of intercity freight demand.' *Highway Research Record* 296, 47-65

National Transportation Act, 14-15-16 Elizabeth II, 1967, Chap. 62

Olson, J. (1972) 'Price discrimination by regulated motor carriers.' *American Economic Review* 62, 395-402

Ontario Economic Council (1976) *Issues and Alternatives: Northern Ontario Development* (Toronto)

Ontario Mineral Review (1974)

Palmer, J. (1973) 'A further analysis of provincial trucking regulation.' *Bell Journal of Economics and Management Science* 4, 655-64

– (1974) 'Taxation by regulation? The experience of the Ontario trucking regulation.' *Logistics and Transportation Review* 10, 207-12

Phillips, A. (1975) *Promoting Competition in Regulated Markets* (Washington DC: The Brookings Institution)

Prabhu, M.A. (1971) 'Freight regulation in Canada.' *McGill Law Journal* 17, 292

Richardson, H.W. (1970) *Regional Economics: A Reader* (London: Macmillan)

Roberts, M.J. (1965) 'Transport costs, pricing and regulation.' In R.J. Meyer, ed., *Transportation Economics* (New York: National Bureau of Economic Research)

Royal Commission on Maritime Claims (1926) *Report* (Ottawa)

Royal Commission on Transportation (1951) *Report* (Ottawa)

Royal Commission on Transportation (1961) *Report* (Ottawa)

Schenker, E. (1969) *Effects of Containerization on Great Lakes Ports*. Special Report No. 2, Center for Great Lakes Studies (Milwaukee)

– (1970) *The Great Lakes Container Dilemma*. Center for Great Lakes Studies (Milwaukee)

Sloss, J. (1970) 'Regulation of motor freight transportation: a quantitative analysis of policy.' *Bell Journal of Economics and Management Science* 1, 327-66.

St Lawrence Seaway Authority, Annual Reports (Ottawa)

Statistics Canada (1973, 72-611) *Labour Costs in Canada 1970* (Ottawa)

Statistics Canada (1974, 95-731 to 95-751) *Census Tract Series B* (Ottawa)

Statistics Canada (1975a, 25-201) *Logging 1973* (Ottawa)

Statistics Canada (1975b, 68-201E) *Principal Taxes and Rates – Federal, Provincial and Local Governments 1974* (Ottawa)

Statistics Canada (1976a, 53-006) *Road Transport Service Bulletin* (Ottawa)

Statistics Canada (1976b, 62-002) *Prices and Price Indexes* (Ottawa)

Statistics Canada (1976c, 26-201) *General Review of the Mineral Industries 1973* (Ottawa)

Statistics Canada (1976d, 31-211) *Products Shipped by Canadian Manufacturers 1971* (Ottawa)

Stigler, G. (1971) 'The theory of economic regulation.' *Bell Journal of Economics and Management Science* 2, 3-19

Straszheim, M.R. (1969) *The International Airline Industry* (Washington DC: The Brookings Institution)

Thompson, W.R. (1965) *A Preface to Urban Economics* (Baltimore: Johns Hopkins Press)

Transport Act, 2 George VI, 1938

Transport Canada (1975) *An Interim Report on Freight Transportation in Canada* (Ottawa)

van den Burg, G. (1969) *Containerization: A Modern Transportation System* (London: Hutchinson)

Warner, Stanley L. (1965) 'Cost models, measurement errors and economies of scale in trucking.' In M. Burstein, A. Cabot, J. Egan, A. Hunter, S. Warner, *The Cost of Trucking: Econometric Analysis* (Dubuque: Wm. C. Brown)

Wilson, G. (1962) *Essays on Some Unsettled Questions in the Economics of Transportation* (Indiana: Indiana University Press)

Wilson, G. and L. Darby (1968) *Transportation on the Prairies*. Royal Commission on Consumer Problems and Inflation (Regina: Government of Saskatchewan)

Woodward, R.S. (1973) 'The iso-outlay function and variable transportation costs.' *Journal of Regional Science* 13, 349-53

- (1974a) 'The capital bias of DREE incentives.' *Canadian Journal of Economics* 7, 161-73
- (1974b) 'Effective location subsidies: an evaluation of DREE industrial incentives.' *Canadian Journal of Economics* 7, 501-10